KDP: Zero

By Antonis Tsagaris

KDP: Zero to Hero

Antonis Tsagaris

Also by Antonis Tsagaris

nonfiction

Merch: Zero to Hero

Android Development for Gifted Primates: A Beginner's Guide

Shake 'Em By The Legs: A Freelancer's Guide to Getting Paid

fiction

Satan, Aliens, Go!

Table of Contents

About the author

Antonis was born in 1980 on the relatively small Mediterranean island of Cyprus, also affectionally known to its inhabitants as the "Golden-Green Leaf", "The Island of Saints", "The Birthplace of Aphrodite" and "This Fucking Place".

After an idyllic childhood of long summers and short, timid winters, he decided that he could be spending his time more productively than rolling in the dirt and eating hawthorn fruits straight off the branch, so he sat down and wrote his first book: a ten-part mini-epic called "Bones", which was about the dinosaur apocalypse, five years before *Jurassic Park* debuted. Take that, Steven "Ooh, I'm such an awesome director" fucking Spielberg.

More exciting stuff you should know about the author of this book, you say? Still not convinced he's a shining beacon of wisdom and grace, you say? *Fine*. He's a Doctor of Dental Surgery (ie. a dentist) and holds a Master of Science in Oral Surgery and Pathobiology. He's also the designer and developer of multiple acclaimed Android apps, a half-decent graphic designer and the principal songwriter for Electric Sound Continuum.

He also likes sucking the marrow of life, which is not nearly as disgusting as it sounds.

Introduction

Writing and publishing a book can be a daunting task. Just ask the millions upon millions of authors that have published books on Amazon's Kindle Store.

Wait. There's something wrong with the previous sentence. My contradiction-detecting gadget from the future is trilling faster than a Geiger counter next to a steaming pile of Godzilla poop.

Here's a better version: writing a decent book, publishing it to acceptable standards and promoting it properly to give it a chance to find its market can be daunting. There—no more trilling.

Let's get one thing straight from the start so that you can get a refund if you bought this book with the wrong expectations: this book is **not** going to help you write a better book. Instead, it assumes that you have already written a half-decent book and that you're looking to publish it on Kindle Direct Publishing, Amazon's platform for self-published authors.

If you're shocked that there's more to becoming a successful self-published author than simply writing a decent (or even an awesome) book and throwing it on Amazon, maybe keep this book. You're gonna need it.

Here are some very important facts you should know from the outset:

- The Kindle store is absolutely flooded with books. There are thousands of them being released each and every week. Writing a book, uploading it on KDP and expecting it to start selling copies is like singing in the shower in the hopes that your apartment has really thin walls through which the CEO of Sony Music that coincidentally lives next door can hear you and, enchanted by your dulcet tones, offer you a contract. I mean, it *could* happen.
- On a similar note, if you hate marketing, stop hating marketing. You'll be spending a lot of time doing it, there's no way around that.
- If you think that writing, formatting, publishing and promoting a book once is hard work, then imagine what it takes to do it multiple times a year—because that's literally what every successful indie publisher is doing.
- If you are working a full-time job, get ready for lots of late nights or early mornings. Or both. It's going to take a lot of hard work and determination to reach a point where you'll be making some decent income from your writing.

The good news is that, just like any other skill, the more you do it, the better you'll become at it. What seems like an insurmountable obstacle on your first launch ("How do I get that coveted #1 New Release badge?") is going to look like child's play by your fifth book release. Remember how mommy had to potty train you for three months when you were a toddler? Of course you don't. It doesn't matter, though, because what's important is that right now you can walk into that toilet and effortlessly take a massive dump with the best of them.

Many of you may ask, "What's so different about this book?" Honestly, I don't know. I guess I swear a lot? And I'm painfully honest? Also, I have no tutorials, courses or personal coaching to peddle, so this book is not just a thinly-disguised, badly-executed excuse to upsell you on that kind of stuff? Yeah, maybe all of the above.

Here's my promise: no over-the-top hype, no slimy upsells, no Paulo Coelho quotes. Just true, down-to-earth, actionable information you can put to good use. And maybe I'll also make you laugh (or cringe so hard you'll explode) a couple of times.

Let's get going.

Chapter 1: So You've Written A Book

Congratulations. Nobody cares.

I'm not saying this to be edgy or an asshole. It's a simple statement of fact. If you want to put my assertion to the test, then do this: create a KDP account. Upload your manuscript and a plain cover with the title of your book in Times New Roman on a white background. Fill all mandatory fields, set a price you think is fair and click 'Submit'. Let me know how that goes.

You see, right now, that breathtaking piece of elegant, transcendent literature that you've been toiling on for years has about as much impact on the world as a badly-written, horribly-punctuated twenty page-long nonfiction booklet about dog training. Thankfully, we can change that.

Here's the first thing you need to do: you need to distance yourself from it. There's only one person in the world to whom this book is special and that's you. So go on, use a mental wrecking ball to demolish the pedestal you've put it on. As far as you're concerned, that book is now a product that you have to sell to an audience—even if the thought of it just made you puke a little in your mouth.

Write to Market

The most important question you have to ask yourself at this point is this: Who am I trying to sell this book to? In self-publishing circles, one phrase you'll hear being uttered constantly is "write to market", ie. find out what the market wants and write *that*. While I agree in concept, in reality, this can turn out to be quite counterproductive.

Yes, finding an underserved market and going after it is Marketing 101. As strange as it may sound to a new author, quite a few self-publishers on KDP are not actually authors. Instead, they are essentially marketers, looking for the next big craze/keyword, finding it and then hiring ghostwriters to write books around what they believe has the potential to sell. It is, as they say, a living. Unfortunately for them, as they become more successful, more like-minded souls zero in on the niche/keyword and then they have to go chase the next big Niche In The Sky to (hire others to) write about.

You may detect a certain amount of disdain in my previous paragraph but I assure you that none of that is intentional. I'm just not personally a fan of this method, for various reasons. Here are two of them

- The resulting books are usually—how can I put this mildly—*shit*. The lack of passion and a distinctive voice usually makes those books a slog to get through. Many ghostwriters are not very proficient in English (hiring a Filippino writer through Upwork is way cheaper than hiring someone in the UK, for example) so you get all sorts of spelling and grammatical errors strewn all through the book.

- Many of these books are created by their 'authors' as a way of funneling their readers towards more expensive training and courses. Again, this leads to shallow, unsatisfying reads that withhold information from you, just to charge you a premium for it later. Feel free to disagree with me on this (and I'm sure that many will) but I think that it's pretty sleazy of someone to sell you a quote-unquote book that's actually their marketing material.

Am I saying that "write to market" is a worthless concept? No—far from it. If you want to have any success, you have to do some research. But to learn more, you'll have to buy my course "Kindle Niche Hunting: Hunting for Niches on Kindle", a value of $2000, now only $297 for a limited time. ACT NOW OR BE MISERABLE FOREVER!

Write to Market 2: BSR

You cannot be a self-published author on Amazon and not know what BSR means.

BSR stands for Best Sellers Rank and you should think of it as the Amazon charts. The smaller the number, the more copies a book is selling, similarly to how the second song in a Top Ten list is selling more copies than the ninth song in the same Top Ten list.

For Kindle books, you can find this number by scrolling down to the Product Details section and checking out the Amazon Best Sellers Rank. It will look something like this

Amazon Best Sellers Rank: #93,402 Paid in Kindle Store

The BSR is an indispensable tool for your research, whether you've already written your book or not. If you've already written a book, you can look at the best-selling books in your genre and see what their covers, descriptions, etc. look like. This will give you an idea as to what readers in your genre expect to see, price-, cover- and description-wise, which is important information to have at hand when you're listing your book or making/ordering your cover. You can even use this info to show targeted ads about your book to people searching for those best sellers on Amazon(more on this later).

I know I said that this book is supposed to teach you how to publish and market a finished manuscript but, since we're discussing BSR, here's a short description of how to use it to help you make a decision about what to write. If you haven't written your book yet, and you're still deciding on a genre/subject matter, you can do a search for your preferred terms and see what comes up. Let's say that you love science fiction but you don't know what you should write about. Should you go for a space opera starring a badass princess in a gold bikini? A first contact story? A Hitchhiker's Guide To The Galaxy-esque sci-fi comedy novel?

In any case, you need to know if there's an audience for what you're about to write. A frequently suggested method for this is to go to the subgenre's Best Sellers list and check the BSRs of the first fifty books on that list. If the first and fiftieth books have very low BSRs, that means that they are selling a lot of copies and that the competition in that subgenre is fierce. At the time of writing, in the Space Opera Science Fiction bestsellers list, the first book has a BSR of 122 (which is VERY good) and the fiftieth book has a BSR of 3340 (still very good). These books (and all other books between them) are selling like hotcakes so clearly there's an audience, but on the other hand, it's going to be a very tough subgenre to break into.

If the first and fiftieth book on a subgenre's best seller's list have very high BSRs, it's a clear sign that there's not a big audience for that particular genre. If, however, the first book in the bestseller list has a very low BSR (which means it's selling a lot) but the fiftieth book has a very high BSR, that means that there's both an audience for books in that subgenre *and* an opportunity for you to break into it. This is the best-case scenario, so start writing that book!

Write to Market 3: OK, A Quick Mention on What You Could Write About

Listen, I know I said that this book would only come in handy after you've already written a book. However, if you still haven't written a book or if you've written a couple of them and want to get ideas for more books, I suggest you ask yourself the following questions

1. **What do I know really well?** Write about that. Your job or that hobby you're really passionate about could be great inspirations for your first or for a future book. I'm a dentist and dentistry is one of the most boring things you can write about. But, trust me, you still want to read my book "You Know The Drill: Demystifying Dentistry" when it comes out.

2. **What am I learning right now?** Writing a book about something you're currently learning may make you feel like a fraud but there's a ton of people out there wishing for simpler, more approachable books—and guess who's the best candidate to teach them? A seasoned pro may know more about the subject than you do, but you have one huge advantage: you know what stumps beginners, and you can laser-focus on those issues in your book. So if you've signed up for a Vue.js or Advanced Photoshop course on Udemy, watch it and take notes. That way, you'll be learning a new skill and taking notes that could later serve as the basis for your book.

Oh, boy. Put down those torches and pitchforks, fellas. It's not fucking Transylvania.

Let me be clear about something: **I'm not saying that you should plagiarize books and courses**. That would be pretty despicable of you and it could also get you into trouble.

What I'm saying is that you should devote *a lot* of time into learning a new skill by watching, listening to and reading multiple courses, Youtube videos, books, podcasts, etc. You should then apply those skills into creating something new. While you're creating that thing, whatever it's going to be, you're going to run into trouble: Photoshop will be an annoying little shit when you try to select a subject. The reverb you inserted into channel 1 will be bleeding into the entire mix. The Android SDK will subvert your expectations and it will work as documented for 20 milliseconds before deciding to crap out because, five days earlier, you decided to descale the kettle.

Cherish the trouble. Cherish the parts you don't understand. When you learn how to deal with that stuff, that's when you'll be able to write a book that teaches other newbies how to get over those problems, written by someone who was, until recently, a newbie himself.

Finally, when you study the subject you want to write about extensively, make sure that your book has a differentiating factor that makes it better than the rest of the pack in at least one way. Make it easier to understand, make it funnier, include models in bikinis on every other page, etc.

If you write fiction (or intend to write fiction), read a lot of books in the genre you're writing in, study the tropes of your preferred genre (it's easy; go to Google and type the name of your genre, followed by the word "tropes") and make sure that you study proper story structure (there's many books on the subject, with some of my favorites being "Save The Cat Writes A Novel" by Jessica Brody, "The Story Grid" by Shawn Coyne, "Plot Gardening" by Chris Fox and "Understanding Show, Don't Tell" by Janice Hardy).

Chapter 2: Preparing your book for publication

Formatting your book

Before we go any further, I'd like to mention something: there's an alternative to formatting your book yourself and that is, predictably, to get someone else to do it for you. Getting someone else to do it for you means that you'll have to pay them. Wouldn't you rather just keep the money and spend it on something worthwhile, like hookers?

And what happens when you write your next book? And the one after that? As Jesus of Nazareth said right before he pushed the Publish button for his book "Putting Demons Into A Bunch Of Swine: Don't Try This At Domus", it's better to teach a man to format his own books than to format a thousand books for him. There: I didn't say it, the Son of God did.

I wouldn't ask you to format your own book if it wasn't a very simple affair. Can you pick your nose? Then you can format your book. If you need any proof of that, let me share a story with you: it was a dark and stormy night, and I was just starting out my self-publishing journey on KDP. My manuscript was complete but now I had to format it, so I went on Amazon and searched for "penis enlargement". Disappointed with the results, I then searched for "how to format my ebook" and decided to buy a book that shall remain unnamed. It claimed to be the complete guide to formatting your book for KDP and it was forty pages long. *That's kinda short* I thought as I clicked the "Buy now with 1-click" button, but what I didn't know was that *about half of that* was a totally irrelevant section (which the author called a "bonus" section) about another, completely unrelated aspect of self-publishing. That's right, he had to pad the book with 20 pages of fluff to get it to the—still pretty goddamn skinny—40 pages guide that it was.

Thankfully, what that doofus taught me in 20-something pages, I can teach you in two.

Here's what you'll need to do:

- Insert page breaks
- Take care of your headings
- Generate a table of contents, if relevant
- Insert any images you may have
- Insert page numbers (this is for formatting paperbacks, which we won't be covering in this book)
- Enter the header text (also for paperbacks, see above)

Keep this in mind: when KDP generates a .mobi file from your document for use on Kindle devices, you don't really get a lot of say in font selection or line spacing. Readers can adjust those things to their liking on their devices, which may sound like a nightmare for the control freaks out there but to me, it's two fewer things to worry about.

You can format your book in any word processing software you prefer, although I like to use Google Docs for my books (I don't even know why I'm paying 10 bucks/month for that MS Office subscription anymore). After you're done, you generate a .docx file and you upload that on KDP.

Inserting page breaks

"What's a page break?" I thought I heard you ask, although that might have been my lower intestine. Sometimes it makes these weird noises that sound like people reading my books and asking me questions. The doctor assured me it's nothing to worry about.

A page break tells the device that's showing your text **where one page ends and another one starts**. It may sound like a small thing but it's the most important part of formatting your book. Before people learn what a page break is, they place the cursor above the text they want to push to the next page and start pressing the Enter key in their word processing software to push it down, until it appears to be on the next page. **That's a very bad idea**. In this case, the rendering software that displays your book on Kindles cannot tell that there's a page break and will treat the space you created by pressing Enter as normal text flow. If you use this method to split your manuscript into pages, the resulting Kindle ebook will look worse than Cthulhu's mama in a Freddy Krueger costume.

Instead, let's say that you've just generated your table of contents and you have the Dedication page following. To make sure that the dedication text is on its own page, as is customary, place the dedication text *directly* below the table of contents, go to the start of the dedication text line and press

- If you're on a Windows / Chrome OS / Linux computer: Ctrl + Enter
- If you're on a Mac: take a sip of your soy latte and press Command + Enter

This will take the dedication text to its own page, but *properly*. Now you know that, whatever the default or user-modified settings of the Kindle device, the dedication will appear on its own page, at the top of it. After you've done this, insert a page break below the dedication text, so that you don't have anything else on the Dedication page.

TIP: If you hate using shortcuts because you took a shortcut and were mugged at gunpoint six years ago, you can insert a page break by

1. Placing your cursor where you want the page break to be inserted
2. Going to the menu bar (the one that says 'File' 'Edit' 'View' etc.) and selecting Insert > Break > Page Break (in Google Docs) or Insert > Page Break (in MS Word)

Taking care of your headings

Do you see that text above this line? The one that says 'Taking care of your headings', which is the title of this section? That's a *Heading 3* in Google Docs.

Headings allow you to split your manuscript into distinct sections, like parts, chapters, subchapters, etc. Headings make the manuscript more scannable, as each heading level takes on a distinct appearance that allows the reader to differentiate between various sections of the manuscript.

Another benefit of using headers is the ability to have a Table of Contents (ToC) automatically generated by your word processing software. Based on the headings you've provided, the software will generate a nested list of your parts, chapters and so on. The items on that list can be clickable if you wish them to be, which you do.

In this very book, the main sections (eg. Introduction, Chapter 1, Chapter 2, etc) are marked as *Heading 1*. Any sections within a chapter are marked as *Heading 2*. Any subsections within a section are marked as *Heading 3*. No prizes for guessing what any further subsections within *those* subsections are marked as.

This explains why this section, 'Taking care of your headings', is styled as a Heading 3.

Chapter 2: Preparing Your Book for Publication is a Heading 1
Formatting Your Book, a subsection within chapter 2, is a Heading 2
Taking Care of Your Headings, a subsection within Formatting Your Book, is a Heading 3

To apply a heading, highlight the text you want to apply the Heading attribute to and

- In **Google Docs**, go to Format > Paragraph Styles > Heading X, where X is the heading style you want to apply.
- In **MS Word**, go to Home > Styles and select the heading style you want

Generate a Table of Contents

If you've already applied your heading styles, generating your ToC is a piece of cake.

- In Google Docs, go to Insert > Table of Contents and select the style of ToC you wish to have (A. with page numbers and no clickable links or B. without page numbers but with clickable links. I suggest that you always use the latter for Kindle eBooks, even though I've noticed that using the first style will also end up creating clickable links in the final ebook). The ToC will be placed at the position where your cursor was.
- In MS Word, go to References > Table of Contents and select your style. Again, the ToC will be placed where your cursor was.

After the ToC has been generated, check it thoroughly.

Inserting images

Sometimes you just gotta insert an image or two in your book, you know? Here's how you do it:

- In Google Docs, go to Insert > Image and select the image you want to place in the document.
- In MS Word, go to Insert > Pictures and select your image

Both programs allow for a variety of relationships between the text and the image, like 'Inline', 'Wrap text' and 'Break text'. They also allow you to resize, reposition and rotate the image. Here's my take on all of this: fuck this shit.

In my experience, trying to effectively manipulate images in a word processing program so that they render correctly on a Kindle device is like trying to milk a cow with your eyelashes; it won't work and, even if it does, you still milked a cow with your eyelashes, you numbnuts. Just place the image somewhere serviceable and save yourself a couple of hours of rage-inducing tinkering. The computer's going to win this one. Just roll with it.

TIP: DO NOT place a lot of pictures in your manuscript. Also, scale down the ones you'll place in the document by using a program like Photoshop, GIMP, etc. You don't want your book's file size to explode because, if you price your book between \$2.99 and \$9.99, Amazon will charge you a delivery fee that gets higher as the size of your manuscript increases.

Getting a cover for your book

It's a oft-repeated rule in the self-publishing community that you should have a high-quality cover for your book because people do actually judge a book by its cover. And, in a massive departure from my contrarian ways, I kind of agree with that assessment.

Stephen King could release a book with just his name, book title and the photo of a poop-smeared wall between them (in fact, I wouldn't be surprised if he already has) and that book would sell like hotcakes. You do not have that luxury. Nobody knows who you are.

And so, we face the ultimate irony: people that can afford expensive covers don't really need them while people who really need expensive covers cannot afford them. OK, I lied. It's not the ultimate irony.

That's not to say that a really nice cover is all you need to sell your book. If I could describe my first two books aurally, it would be the sweet sound of chiming cash registers. My third book, which had the nicest cover of the three by far, would be the reverberating sound of a turd plopping into the toilet.

If 'nice' simply refers to the cover being esthetically-pleasing, then 'nice' does not cut it. Yes, it should be pretty, no doubt. But it should also

- Be genre-appropriate
- Be legible
- Not cost a million dollars

The genre-appropriate cover

You can have the most beautiful cover in the world and a manuscript that puts every other attempt in its genre to shame, but if your military sci-fi epic has a retro cover that shows a girl in a polka-dot dress standing on her toes, sniffing a hibiscus flower on a sidewalk in London, you may want to prepare yourself for disappointment.

You cover probably needs a huge spaceship coming out of a wormhole, space guns ablaze. Or, alternatively, a couple of dudes and a dudette in combat gear, holding huge guns, shooting at some unseen threat while the testosterone emanating from their bodies slowly suffocates the surrounding flora and fauna.

Here's a pretty obvious tip: take a look at other books in your genre and see what the readers of the genre expect to see on the cover. Then, give it to them. Sounds too boring and predictable? Too bad. You know what's *not* boring when it's predictable? *Sales*, motherfucker.

Are there any exceptions to this rule? I guess, but I cannot really think of one right now—which, if you ask me, says it all.

Nonfiction books will give you more latitude to experiment with covers, although you'll still find that some genres have their own conventions. What should the cover of a self-help book that contains meditation techniques look like? I'm not sure, though I imagine that it probably involves bonsais, people sitting cross-legged and/or babbling brooks. A ketogenic diet book cover will probably involve some plates with food in them or some douchette looking at you with a Stepford Wife smile surrounded by some plates with food in them.

The legible cover

Never break this rule: make sure that the user can read, at the very least, your book's title from the thumbnail in Amazon's search results. If they are able to read the subtitle too, that's even better.

You may be thinking, "Why does it matter? The title and subtitle and series name and edition and who wrote it and the price and the publishing house and everything else is written right next to the thumbnail."

Exactly.

There's so much noise in the text next to the thumbnail that it's much easier for a prospective reader to just read the title and subtitle straight from the book cover.

I don't care if you have the most amazing illustration of a naked lady riding a dragon, with a brewing storm in the background. If I can't read *"The Dragontitty Chronicles, Book One: Revenge is a Dish Breast Served Cold"* straight off your cover, I probably won't bother with your book.

The affordable cover

How much should you pay for your cover?

As much as you can **reasonably** afford. I hate this weird trend that's been making the rounds in the self-publishing community that says "You know, if you can't afford a nice cover right now, just save up for six months and, when you can afford it, order a $1000 cover from Master Artist So-and-So."

No. Just no.

You can put your book out there right now and have it work for you on Amazon as an asset. Six months? Let's put those six months into perspective: even if you live to be a hundred years old, you'll only live two hundred six-month-long periods. I apologize for getting all grimdark here but the clock is ticking.

"Hmm.." interjects my lower intestine again (or maybe it's really you this time), "then what am I supposed to do? You say I need a nice cover, but you also say that I shouldn't wait to be able to pay for one. Are you off your meds again?"

Well, what I say, Lower Intestine, *if that's your real name,* is that there alternatives to either having a modern impressionistic masterpiece with flawless typography or yellow Comic Sans on a black background on the front of your book. Don't get me wrong: if you can afford it without it placing a huge strain on your budget (if, for example, you've been self-publishing with some success for more than a year) then go for the extravagant cover. But not everybody can do that.

For the rest of you, this is what you can do.

The Do-It-Yourself Cover

But probably not *completely* by yourself.

If you have some graphic design skills (eg. you're pretty good with Illustrator and Photoshop and you know what the pathfinder and/or a gradient map is) then it is quite reasonable for you to attempt to do it completely by yourself. That's what I do, but I've been using Adobe's suite for years.

Even then, designing a book cover is quite different from designing a logo or a birthday card, even if most design principles will apply to all of these cases. But I would say go for it and see what you get out of it.

If, however, you've never drawn a circle or desaturated a photo before, *PLEASE STOP AND THINK OF THE CHILDREN.*

What happens next depends on the kind of book you've written. If you've written a nonfiction one, just go to Canva (https://www.canva.com) and use one of the hundreds of templates they offer to create a customized version of a professionally-designed cover. Just be careful: don't get cocky and suddenly think you're a designer. **Leave the colors, fonts, and layouts alone**. They were chosen by a pro for a reason. For reference, here's a fitness-oriented one I knocked out in thirty seconds:

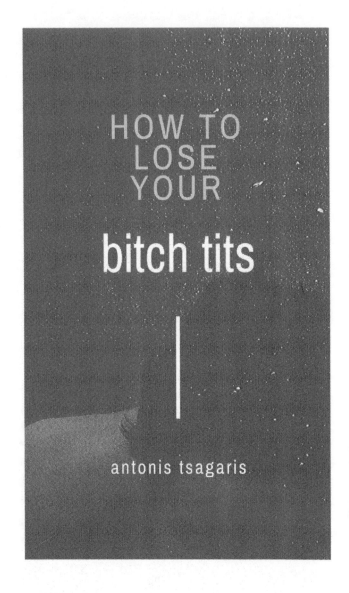

If I really wanted to, I could have gone to Unsplash (https://unsplash.com), the motherlode of royalty-free photos, and downloaded a more appropriate photo to load into the template. As I've already mentioned, if you have no graphic design experience it's best to stick close to the templates and resist the temptation to tinker a lot with them.

By the way, you can use Canva to make covers for fiction books too. It currently offers templates for romance, thriller and science fiction book covers, as well as a less well-defined 'fiction' category. I'm not a great fan of their fiction templates but go check them out, you may find something you like. Here's another one I knocked out in a minute for an imaginary romantic comedy book:

'DISGUSTINGLY EARNEST'

HOW DO I TELL HER

I REALLY NEED TO USE THE TOILET RIGHT NOW?

by STEVE BIZZARO

The best part about Canva, especially if you're strapped for cash, is that you can use it for free and even export your work without having to pay a dime. They also offer a premium plan, which unlocks a ton of photos, fonts and other assets, and a pay-as-you-go choice, which lets you purchase specific pro-tier assets for use in your designs.

Another benefit of Canva is that, since you'll be making the covers, you can keep a consistent style between books in the same series, something which is harder to do with the other option I'm about to suggest.

Premades

Premades are exactly what their name suggests: premade covers, waiting for a title and author name to be added to them.

To me, this is the way to go for fiction books, if you don't have a big budget. They are not usually that expensive (prices usually range between $100-200) and, depending on the vendor, they usually look very nice.

I am not going to suggest any vendors because any links I may provide can become outdated very fast (in fact, I just heard two links screeching and evaporating in the distance while I was writing the last sentence—and have you heard a link screeching its way into oblivion? It'll give you nightmares for weeks). What you should do is go to Google and search for "premade covers" + your genre name. You'll have no trouble finding covers, trust me.

Naturally, not everything is peaches and sunshine in Premadecoverland, Authortopia: if you intend to write a series and not just a standalone novel, you may have some trouble with inconsistency between the covers of the books in your series. Usually, you'd want the covers in a series to look at least vaguely similar, with a unified art style and typography, something that may not be possible with premades, as you won't have any control over the artistic direction of the covers (other than adding your title and name). In that case, you have a couple of choices:

- Choose some covers that look similar, and hope nobody notices that your main character had a tattoo, anal bleaching, liposuction, TRX training and a face transplant between book one and book two in the series (or, hey, just make it part of the story! You know what they say about lemons and lemonade!)
- Go to a premade covers site and see if they offer a "Series" section. I know that Paper & Sage do it (https://www.paperandsage.com/premade-category/series/) but as I said, it's better if you do a Google search. For all I know, Paper & Sage could have started selling papier-mâché sage-infused dildos in the time it took me to figure out how to spell papier-mâché.

Are you going to edit that?

Yes, of course you will. Never release first drafts, please. If you're thinking of releasing the first draft of a book, bear in mind that the most appropriate place for you to release it would be straight into a tornado.

The question is not whether editing will happen or not. The *real* question is who it will be done by. Maybe it will be done by you. Maybe it will be done by an editor or even multiple ones.

Keep in mind, especially if this is your first rodeo, that editors are expensive. And there are many different kinds of editing that they perform: *line editing, copy editing, developmental editing* and *quantum editing* (one of those editing types is made-up). Established authors would be crazy not to go with a professional editor (or team of editors). Less well-known authors or authors with a very limited budget? Bitter wars have been fought online over this matter, and while the winners in some battles have been clear (mainly because their opponent had to stop replying to the thread and go to bed), the outcome of the war itself is not yet defined.

Some authors think you'd be mad to release a book without at least some sort of editor going over it first. They think that just because you haven't had an editor go through the book with a fine-tooth comb and sort out all issues related to story development, grammar, syntax and then suggest extensive revisions as well as burning your book on a square and starting from scratch is going to let paragraph/sentence hybrids like the one I'm writing now slip through the cracks.

Other authors think that editors are a waste of time. One author, whose books I really enjoy and who clearly knows what he's talking about, has mentioned in at least two of his self publishing-related books that manuscripts that he has had professionally edited ended up having more mistakes in them upon publication than the books that he had edited himself. To be honest, while I believe him that that was the case, I also think that this particular incident was an outlier.

OK. Enough about what other people think. You bought this book to get my opinion, and here's my take (be careful, because it's pretty hot): if I can do my own editing and consistently get reviews about how well-written my books are, then you can do your own editing, at least for your first few books, especially if English is your first language. Because it certainly isn't mine.

If you hadn't guessed by the name on the cover by now, English is not my first language. Greek is. This means that I hadn't been exposed to English in any significant way until third grade, which means that I learned my first word of English at age... let's see...

(Computing...)

(Computing...)

(Computing...)

(Sorry, I'm bad at math in *any* language)

(Computing...)
(Computing...)
(Computing...)

... age 9. If you're from an English-speaking country, you have the advantage of nine years of experience that I never got, which you received during your formative years. Not to mention your everyday experience of using the language to converse with everybody around you.

That's why I get pissed off whenever I see you write "Your so funny!" or "Loose the attitude" on the internet.

What follows is some tough love

- You shouldn't make basic syntax and grammar mistakes if you think of yourself as a writer.
- You should know how to structure your prose into sentences, paragraphs and chapters.
- You should be able to put together a coherent sentence without outside help.
- You should study story structure and strive for uninterrupted flow, consistency of tone and believable character arcs. Craft is important.

If you, like me, were banging hot chicks left and right during late elementary and all through high school and never had time to learn how to spell, guess what: it's time to learn. Or download Grammarly.

Software Killed The Editor Star (Although Not Really)

In case you didn't know, there's software that will highlight your spelling mistakes, suggest corrections and apply them with a click. Grammarly (https://www.grammarly.com) will do that, and much more, for you. You can use Grammarly for free for basic writing corrections or you can spend the small-to-medium bucks and have it help you fix (according to their website, at least)

- Inconsistent writing style
- Unclear sentence structure
- Overused words
- Ineffective vocabulary
- Hedging language
- Impoliteness
- Insensitive or non-inclusive language. What a bunch of pussies.
- Inappropriate tone or formality level
- Plagiarism

I've been using the free version for ages and it never fails to catch my typos, although I see no reason to splurge out on the premium version.

Grammarly is not the only game in town if you're interested in software that'll improve your writing. ProWritingAid (https://prowritingaid.com) will also check your grammar, offer you synonyms from a thesaurus to help you avoid echoing, offer context-sensitive style suggestions and more. It will also generate very helpful reports about your manuscript. Here are some screenshots from their site that illustrate how impressive their analysis can get

He walked across the room quickly and answered the door.

The irony is that I am not adverse to this new world.

The classroom was very full of boisterous children rushing to collect their coats and b

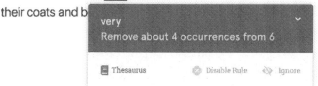

She peered through the hollow tube.
He stepped out on the frozen ice.

It's some seriously impressive technology and, even if you're going to be using an editor anyway, it doesn't hurt to deliver a mostly clean manuscript so that the editor can focus on the stuff that the software cannot check.

Finally, always remember that Google is your friend. A creepy friend with a mustache that always watches from a distance waiting to make his move, but a friend nevertheless. If you have any questions about the correct use of idiomatic expressions, spelling, syntax, etc. just type the expression, word or sentence in the search field and see what comes up.

Alright.

At this point, you should have a nice cover, an edited manuscript and a formatted book file saved in .docx format, which is what KDP prefers. It's time for a martini. In the next chapter, we'll start going through the publishing process together.

Chapter 3: Publishing your masterpiece on KDP

Your book has been written, edited, formatted and Salvador Dalí's great-grandson has prepared the most amazing cover for you. It's time to take the plunge and put it up on the Kindle store for people to buy.

At this point, some people get cold feet. What if it isn't good enough? What if people send me messages telling me how much I suck? What if I get a one-star review on Amazon? WHAT IF MY MAIN CHARACTER LEFT THE OVEN ON IN CHAPTER 17 AND ALL BOOKS IGNITE SHORTLY AFTER RELEASE, BURNING DOWN ALL OF MY READERS' HOMES IN THE PROCESS?

Yes, that's how ridiculous you sound. I'm not saying that you should release crap into the world (unless it comes out of your butthole. In that case, sure, go ahead). I'm just saying that once you've done your best to craft something that you're proud of, don't keep it on your hard disk. Because, here's the deal: whatever you release, you're going to get people telling you that it, and you along with it, suck more than a black hole-powered vacuum cleaner. You *will* get 1-star reviews on Amazon. And if everybody let that stop them from releasing a book, the only thing we'd have to read would be the entrails of chickens, which stinks almost as bad as reading 50 Shades of Grey.

I hope that the pep talk helped because it's time to publish, mister/lady.

First steps

If you don't have an account on KDP yet, go to https://kdp.amazon.com and create one. You can use the Amazon account you already have for shopping or for performing other business on Amazon (for example Merch by Amazon, in which case you go grab this book's sibling Merch: Zero to Hero https://www.amazon.com/dp/B07GGYH7YS, thanks, you're welcome, you won't regret it)

Once you're logged in, you'll see the **Create New Title** section. Click on **Kindle eBook** to get started.

Selecting your book's language

This is pretty self-explanatory. You won't be able to select any language in existence (for example, Greek is not in the list and neither is Klingon. Baktag!) but there are quite a few to select from.

Ok, quick side note: I may be a Star Trek fan but I don't know any Klingon, so I went to find an appropriate insult to use in the last sentence. Imagine my joy when I discovered that one

Klingon insult, **hab sosli' Quch**, means "Your mother has a smooth forehead".

Entering your title and subtitle

Next, you enter your book's title and subtitle.

I imagine that you already have a title (and maybe even subtitle) for your book that you're wedded to, so I'm not going to try and convince you to change it. *However*, what if you need to?

I'm not really talking about fiction here. I'm sure that you're perfectly capable of coming up with a title for your paranormal werewolf romance or high fantasy epic. If you're not, I'm like an automatic generator for this sort of thing, so drop me an email and I'll hook you up. Here are a few that I'll come up on the spot right now:

- Paranormal Werewolf Romance: 'Blood Moon Rising', 'Canine Kiss Your Lips?', 'Howl Deep Is Your Love', 'Sanguine Intentions'
- High Fantasy Epic: 'The Bells Of Calabre', 'Master Of The Watchtower', 'The Sentinel On The Threshold', 'A Song Of The Highlands'

I could keep going all day.

My point is, genre fiction titles have a specific mood and ring to them that you can zero in to, especially if you're a fan of the genre you're writing in. Obviously, I'm being silly with a few of the titles in the werewolf romance genre but a couple of them could be actual book titles (not sure if they actually are).

With nonfiction, you have to be more careful. This is one of those cases where you can be too smart for your own good. To have an effective title with maximum impact, keep the following in mind

- **Keep it short.** It's a title. You have six words, max.
- **Be absolutely clear about your book's content and theme**. The subtitle may come in handy for this purpose, as it allows you to keep your title short and snappy while you expand a little more in the sub. If your book is about yoga, include that word somewhere in the title or subtitle.
- **Avoid overly creative titles.** Nobody is buying your book for the smart pun on the cover. Nobody wants to decode an inside joke for people in the know to even understand what the book is about.
- **Do NOT keyword stuff the title and subtitle.** Keyword stuffing refers to the practice of placing a lot of (sometimes) irrelevant and (always) unnecessary words in the title and subtitle of your book to increase its visibility when people perform searches on Amazon. It's a stupid idea and it'll make your book look like amateur hour. There's a place for you to enter your keywords. It's not here.

Keep in mind that I've written a book called "Android Development for Gifted Primates: A Beginner's Guide" and slapped a banana on the cover. It still works because:

1. The main subject—Android development—is right there on the title. The subtitle also lets the prospective buyer know that the book is meant for beginners.
2. Everybody loves bananas.

Sure, you can have some fun with your titles. Just don't confuse your future customers for the sake of patting yourself on the back.

Is it part of a series?

If your book is part of a series, enter your series name and the position of this specific book in the series. The series name will show up in the title text, in parentheses. For example, if your book is called 'Justice For Antra' and you enter the series name as 'The Falconer Chronicles' and the series number as '2', then what will show up in the search results and in the product page is

Justice For Antra (The Falconer Chronicles 2)

This will also create a section below the book description area called "Books In This Series", which will showcase all books that are part of your series. This is a great promotional tool, as readers won't have to go looking for other titles in the series.

Edition number, Author and Contributors

These are pretty self-explanatory, so I won't go into them. With the exception of the author's name, which is a compulsory field, the other fields are optional.

Description

Entire books have been written and 5-hour courses have been taught about the importance of the description you post on your book's sale page on Amazon. And yet, everybody keeps half-assing it, grudgingly writing a synopsis of their book's story before slamming the laptop shut with the kind of hatred you normally reserve for people that honked at you prematurely at the traffic lights.

I've read those books and I've gone through some of the courses and, while I'm not going to pretend that I can condense *everything* that they taught me in this chapter, I can at least promise that you'll leave this chapter armed with the skills to craft a description that can make a difference to your sales.

Things to avoid

The first thing to keep in mind is that **your book's description shouldn't be your book's synopsis**. You can include vague references to plot elements that happen early on in the book and also references to characters and setting, but what's going to kill your description faster than a fart kills the mood on Valentine's Day is a boring, point-by-point recounting of your book's plot.

First of all, why would you spoil any part of your story? Your job is to intrigue them and to hook them in such a way that they will want to read the book to find out what happens for themselves. This means that each sentence in your description (and *especially* the opening one) should hook them and then pass the mantle to the next sentence, which should also act as a hook. **This will finally bring them to the last line of your description, which should be a call to action**. I call this the Hooker Method.

OK, no, I don't. But I'm serious about the rest of it.

Another thing you should **avoid is big blocks of text**. Space out your sentences and paragraphs and give them some white space to breathe in. It's almost a certainty that a customer browsing on Amazon for his next book will be intimidated by an impenetrable wall of text.

More stuff to avoid: **mentioning a lot of character names and unnecessary details**. I know it took you six months to write your novel and that, after all that time, you have an affinity for those characters but the prospective reader doesn't know who these people are and they are likely to get confused by it. Mention your main character's name and maybe the major antagonist's name and that's it. And if the overuse of names is a no-no, the inclusion of surnames is a no-no-no-you-don't-love-me-and-I-know-now. Go ahead and have a blast mentioning that your main character is of Irish descent and that his full name is Patrick O'Lasergun, but do it in the book.

Things to consider doing

I've mentioned several things that you should avoid when writing your description, but here are some things that you should consider doing.

To start with, let me repeat two points from the Avoid section

- Use the Hooker Method. Yeah, I've decided to adopt it as the official term.
- Space out your text so that it looks more spread out and has more room to breathe. It's way more appealing to someone that's browsing for new books to be able to scan the copy quickly. Spread out text with careful formatting is more important than you think.

Here are a couple more things you should consider

- Make sure that the tone of the description fits the tone of the book. Don't write an overly serious description for a book that's lighthearted and fun and, conversely, don't make butt jokes in the description of "Dealing With The Loss of a Loved One: Grief, Redefined."
- If you're writing nonfiction, don't think that you're off The Hook. You should still have a strong opening line that will get your readers' attention, and you should still guide them towards your call to action, ie. the buy button, with every subsequent line. However, in contrast to fiction descriptions, nonfiction

descriptions NEED to have bullet points. Don't confuse the bullet points of your description for the table of contents of your book. That's not what they are. Instead, **bullet points should describe the various benefits that the reader will obtain from reading your book**. Ideally, they shouldn't describe the route to obtaining those benefits so as to pique the reader's curiosity and increase the chances of making a sale.

Formatting is important so it gets its own section

Formatting is one of those things that's easy to overdo, so just select three things you want to apply to your text and use those. I suggest using variations of

- **Size**: to create dominance and separation between different sections
- **Font weight**: to emphasize the really important parts. I'm mainly referring to bolding the text.
- **Bullet points**: for lists of features, benefits etc, especially in descriptions for nonfiction works.

You can also use italics *sparingly* for attributions of reviews, eg.

"Best book ever!!"
-The New York Times

"I've taken diarrheas with better structure than this disaster"
-The Washington Post

Don't underline stuff. It just looks bad.

You can add formatting to your text by using HTML tags. It's very easy to do, even if you haven't used HTML before. HTML tags are entities that you place around the text you want to style. For example, if you wanted to bold your text, you'd place it inside an opening and a closing **bold** tag, like this

<b> I just bolded some text and I liked it </b>

<b> is the opening tag. It defines the beginning of the text that's to be bolded.
</b> is the closing tag. It defines the end of the text that's to be bolded.

The text between the tags will be bolded. The result will be this:

I just bolded some text and I liked it

PRO-TIP
Remember to always use closing tags. If you don't, you're going to get some unexpected results. One time, I forgot to close a heading tag and a cow fell from the sky and obliterated my Honda Jazz. You've been warned.

At the time of writing, you can get the complete list of supported HTML tags at this link:
https://kdp.amazon.com/en_US/help/topic/G201189630

If you don't want to write HTML, you can use one of the many what-you-see-is-what-you-get KDP description formatters on the web. Whenever I'm having a crisis of confidence and I'm feeling vulnerable and alone, I use Dave Chesson's misleadingly-named Amazon Book Description Generator (it won't generate a description, it'll just let you format it) over at https://kindlepreneur.com/amazon-book-description-generator/

This works like a regular text editor and it will let you highlight sections of your text and apply your formatting to them without having to write a single HTML tag. When you're done, you can click "Generate My Code" and the text, with all formatting applied in HTML, will appear in a text box underneath the button. Copy and paste that text in the description field of your ebook and you're done.

Description case studies

Before I move on to the next section, I'd like to discuss a couple of my own descriptions on Amazon. The first one, for "Android Development for Gifted Primates: A Beginner's Guide", was the first book description I ever wrote, before I studied any copywriting techniques. It's remains unchanged to this day.

The second one is for my novel "Satan, Aliens, Go!". I wrote two descriptions for it, one that I kept for a month and then a second one that's still on Amazon at the time of writing. You'll find both of them pasted below.

Description for "Android Development for Gifted Primates: A Beginner's Guide"

Tired of dry, humorless, life-sucking coding books that feel like they were written by an automaton called Automax-201421?

Me too. That's why this book takes a different approach!

In this very opinionated book about Android development, geared towards beginners, you will learn, among other things

- how to create a user interface by using XML

- how to make that user interface interactive

- how to start background services

- how to facilitate communication between various Android components by using Intents and Broadcast Receivers

- why King Kong should not be able to produce actual excrement **BUT THE GOVERNMENTS KEEP LYING TO US ABOUT IT**

-

> how people debugged their Android apps in the
> trenches of World War I

...and much more.

Written in a very serious and dryly technical manner by Antonis
Tsagaris, this tome of celestial wisdom is meant for beginners and
is rated R for strong language and mild sexuality.

Antonis is the Android developer for codehouse five, a company
specializing in web and Android development. Check out
Karkoona, Looxie, and Veterondo in the Play Store to see some
of his work in action. Most of his apps have been featured in
some Apps of the Week/Month/Year list or another in
world-renowned publications such as TechRadar, The Times of
India, PhoneArena, Android Police and many more.

Antonis enjoys souvlaki, hiking, salivary glands (it's a thing) and
talking about himself in the third person.

DISCUSSION

I got really lucky with this one. First of all, I screwed up with
the formatting of the opening line and made the text huge.
Turns out, that wasn't such a bad thing. Also, the description
formatter I used added a lot of line breaks, which kept the
description text from appearing too dense. And did you see
those bullet points? Sure, the first four are

Table-of-Contents-like but the last two are batshit insane, hinting at the tone of the book itself. Now, when someone reads the first of many fart jokes in the book, they won't feel cheated. The description is missing a call to action (for example, a last sentence saying "Buy it now!") so maybe that's something I'll be adding in the future.

If you're wondering why I haven't changed this description yet, it's because it's effective. The book gets a lot of organic sales and it does great when I advertise it through Amazon Advertising.

Description for "Satan, Aliens, Go!: A novel"

ORIGINAL DESCRIPTION

When mysterious aliens mount a half-assed invasion against the Earth, only one kinda-man can save humanity from sorta-extinction.

Employing the help of his best-buddy-come-reluctant-sidekick Occam, Satan must sneak back into Hell to steal a glorious MacGuffin that potentially has the power to send the aliens packing.

Will Satan's childhood friend, Cthulhu, come to his aid? Will current master of Hell and former victim of Satan's bullying, Baal, forgive him for betraying everybody's trust four years ago? And will Occam's chronic inability to deal with anything more stressful than a spa treatment ever subside?

CURRENT DESCRIPTION

Uh-oh. The aliens are here...

..and they won't leave until they've captured every single human on the planet.

Meanwhile, in a dark room in LA, Satan is rewatching his favorite show when he hears someone banging on his door to bring him news of the invasion.

Together, they set off on an epic journey that will take them through Hell and back. Literally.

Will our heroes be able to stop the aliens from assimilating the human race? And what will they have to sacrifice if they hope to succeed?

A hilarious, fast-paced romp through spacetime with a heart of gold!

You'll fall in love with this funny, heartwarming story of invading aliens, lost love and newfound hope, because not every science fiction book has to be about huge, warring battleships and high-intensity mega-lasers.

Get it now!

DISCUSSION

Here's the power of a good description: before I changed the original description, the only time I made any sales was on the

68

day of a $0.99 promotion. When the promos stopped, the sales stopped, even though I was constantly running Amazon Advertising ads on the book. After I changed the description to the new one, I sold 8 books at $3.99 in a week. Sure, it's not a life-changing amount of sales, but it's infinitely better than before.

The original description has no formatting applied. It's just three plain paragraphs of text. It thinks it's too smart. It contains a lot of character names. And weirdly, for such a short description, it gives too much of the plot away, foraying into the second half of the book at a certain point.

I wrote the second one after I'd studied copywriting for ads and book descriptions. It's got a short opening line that leads straight into the second line of the description. The text is spread out and easy to scan and a bolded line signifies the end of the (intentionally) vague plot synopsis and the transition into pure sales copy. And obviously, it has the obligatory "Get it now!" call to action at the very end of the description.

The results speak for themselves.

Publishing rights

This is an easy one: did you write the book yourself (or own the rights to it, anyway)? Or are you trying to publish Moby Dick with a sweet cover and make some quick moolah?

You can actually publish public domain works on the Kindle store but you should be aware of a couple of things

1. Amazon won't like it if you try to take the public domain text, do some super-quick formatting and throw it on the store, especially if a free version of that work already exists on Amazon. They want you to provide some "differentiation", and the only things they consider to be differentiation are **unique translations**, **text that is uniquely annotated**, or **text that's illustrated**.

2. When you publish a public domain work, you only receive a 35% royalty from any sales you make.

If you're publishing a book that you own the rights to, depending on the price you set for the book (more on this in the Pricing section), you can receive up to a 70% royalty from your sales.

Keywords

The next section on the form is Keywords, and you're given seven text fields in which to enter your (gasp!) keywords.

The first thing I should clear up about the entire thing is that **a keyword does not refer to a single word**. A keyword could be a single word, but usually, a keyword refers to a phrase.

Confused? Let me give you an example: say I want to fill in the seven keywords for this very book. Keywords help users discover your book since they are taken into account, along with other factors, when a customer performs a search on Amazon. To come up with these words, you have to think about what a customer would search for on Amazon that would lead them to your book.

Off the top of my head, here's seven keywords I would use

Kindle Direct Publishing book

How to self-publish my book on Amazon

Self-publishing guide

Sell ebooks on amazon

Self-publishing for beginners

Selling books on Kindle

Kdp book

As you can see, none of them are single words, which is exactly how it works. You need to be very specific and, with the Kindle Store becoming as saturated as it is nowadays, even this amount of specificity may not be able to provide any visibility for your book, especially in highly-competitive categories.

To understand what I mean, let's perform a search for each keyword on the list and see how many results come up:

Kindle Direct Publishing book: 861 results

How to self-publish my book on Amazon: 95 results

Self publishing guide: over 10,000 results

Sell ebooks on Amazon: over 1000 results

Self-publishing for beginners: over 2000 results

Selling books on Kindle: over 10,000 results

Kdp book: over 4000 results

With the exception of a quite long one ("how to self-publish my book on Amazon"), the results are not that encouraging. However, you should take comfort in the fact that keywords are not the only thing that Amazon's algorithm takes into account when ranking the results of a search. Nobody knows *exactly* how it works, but click-through rate, consistency of sales, relevancy, etc. are other metrics that influence where a book appears in search.

Secondly, and more importantly, if you're counting on organic discovery of your books to make some decent income on KDP, you might as well buy a lottery ticket, burn it, place its ashes in a clear acrylic box and hope for some localized reversal of entropy to bring the molecules of the ticket back to its original, unburnt form so that it can win the lottery.

Unless you're writing in some underserved niche that just happened to go big yesterday, you're going to need to run ads to your book pages. Later in the book, we'll look into Amazon Advertising and how it can help you sell your books.

Categories, Or: African Dramas and Plays

Next, KDP lets you choose two categories in which your book will be placed. This is pretty straightforward and there are no filthy tricks or bizarre gaming of the system to be done.

LOL.

That paragraph you just read? Yeah, it's bull— just wipe it off your mind because I'm about to tell you what actually happens.

Yes, you can choose up to two categories in which your book will be placed. Let's use this book as an example. By drilling down into the selection tree, I found two categories that my book could conceivably fit into:

- Nonfiction > Self-help > Creativity
- Nonfiction > Business and Economics > Entrepreneurship

They are not perfect fits for my book but there's nothing more appropriate to select, so they'll have to do, right? Right?

Not so fast, baby!

First of all, you can rest assured that there are far more appropriate categories for you to select, but Amazon, like the sneaky little douche that it is, prefers to hide them from you, presumably for the lolz.

Here's how you can find a much more appropriate category for your book:

1. **Cut a hole in a box.**
2. **Put your junk in that box.**
3. **Search for books that are in your genre**. In my case, I went ahead and performed a search for "kdp publishing"
4. **Select one that has the same subject matter as yours or is very similar in content. Make sure that the book you select has been on Amazon for at least a month or so**. I went for "*KDP - How to self-publish your book on Amazon - The beginner's guide - The key elements for independent (indie) author success (Financial Freedom Beginners Guides 4)*". I know. I wish I was kidding but that's the full title of the book. You can fill turkeys for a century of Thanksgivings with all that stuffing.
5. **Scroll down to the Product Details section and see in which categories it's placed.** They are likely to be far more appropriate for your book than the junk Amazon makes you select during your book's setup. The interesting categories are the ones where the book you are browsing is ranking highly at. For example, if the book ranks #1256 in Category A, #89 in Category B and #2 in Category C, make a note of Category C and proceed to the next step.
6. To see the full category classification, click on the category and when the next page loads, take a look on the left. For example, I clicked on *Authorship* and on

the next page I discovered that the fill classification is **Kindle Store > Kindle ebooks > Reference > Writing, Research and Publishing Guides > Publishing and Books > Authorship**. **Write down the category in this format**, you'll need it in a bit.

7. **Repeat this procedure with another book**. Choose other categories that are appropriate for your book, making sure to select the ones where this book ranks highly.

8. **Before you do anything else, go ahead and publish your book on Amazon**.

9. After your book has been published on the Kindle Store, send an email to Amazon by going at https://kdp.amazon.com/en_US/contact-us and selecting "Manage books on your bookshelf". Then select "Send us an email" and send them an email asking for your book to be included in the categories you've chosen (in the format I've shown you above). Do not overdo it: ask them to place you in three categories you've selected and do it nicely.

10. **Take your junk out of the box**, you perv.

There's a very good reason we're going through this process: we're selecting categories in which your own book can rank highly. Your book is way more likely to reach number one in a very narrow category than in a more general one. For example, your nocturnal Victorian midget thriller is more likely to rank highly in **Fiction > Thrillers > Victorian Thrillers > Nocturnal Victorian Thrillers > Nocturnal Victorian Thrillers With Midget Protagonists** than Fiction >

Thrillers. It helps if, while selecting categories, you compare the book's overall rank (BSR) in the Kindle Store with its ranking in a subcategory.

To make this clearer, let me give you an example: if a book is #1 in a subcategory and #50,000 overall in the Kindle Store, that means that it reached #1 in the subcategory while selling a couple of copies per day (because that's what a book with a BSR of #50,000 is selling, approximately). This also means that if you release your book and have your mom and dad buy it, you can probably get to #1 in a subcategory yourself.

You may be thinking "What the hell do I care if I get to #1 in a subcategory? I'm not here for the bragging rights, I'm here to make money."

What you may not know is that if you rank highly in any category, and if your book is recently released, you may get a nice yellow/orange badge on your book, calling it a "#1 New Release". This badge is visible on your sales page, in the search results, in also-boughts, etc. Basically everywhere. And if you manage to reach #1 in any subcategory, your book will get a badge saying "#1 Best Seller in…", followed by the category you are #1 in. I shouldn't need to tell you that this improves the visibility of your book and drives downloads and sales.

The #1 Best Seller and #1 New Release badges are so sought-after by indie authors on the Kindle Store that sometimes they place their books in ridiculously irrelevant, low-competition categories just so they can get these badges. The funniest one I've come across is this:

MEMORY IMPROVEMENT:
Easy Way to Learn Faster
and Remember More...
› Steve Jones

★★★★☆ 9

 in African
Dramas & Plays
Kindle Edition
$4.75

If your memory improvement book is #1 in African Dramas & Plays, you may need to reconsider your life choices. Please, don't do this. It's ridiculous, it's clearly trying to game Amazon's storefront (which is something they don't take very kindly to) and I'm pretty sure that you can find a more appropriate low-competition category to place you book into.

Age and grade range

Next, you get to select the age and grade range for your book. This is optional but go ahead and select a range if you are writing children's' books or books meant for students.

Pre-order

If you're still writing a book or just want the book you've already prepared to be released at some future date, you can select the "Pre-order" option.

Putting up a pre-order while you're still writing your book has the following pros:

- You are setting a deadline for yourself. This will force you to sit your ass down and write a thousand words a day, even with the tantalizing Netflix devil sitting on your left shoulder whispering "Go on, watch another Stranger Things episode, it's only 45 minutes" in your ear. Begone, demon!
- You can start making sales immediately. If your cover and description are good, and if you promote the pre-order, people can start buying your book, which will be delivered to their Kindle devices automatically on the specified release date.

- Making sales before the release date means that you'll appear on other people's also-boughts (the section that says "People that bought this book also bought so and so") right on release. This is a powerful marketing tool since Amazon is showing your book to people that are probably interested in it.

PRO-TIP

'Also-boughts' is a section on a Kindle book page and its location on the page is defined by the Schroedinger equation, ie. Amazon will change its location and even existence so often you'll never know if it was actually a thing to begin with. Well, I've collapsed that particular wave function (sorry for speaking in Nerdish, it's just this paragraph, I promise) and I can confirm that it actually exists, sometimes, and that when it exists it's somewhere on the page.

To balance out the pros, here are the cons:

- If you fail to meet the release deadline (you need to upload your finished manuscript five days before the release date you've set), Amazon will bitchslap you so hard you'll start enjoying *Transformers: Revenge of the Fallen* unironically. Effectively, they will remove your ability to set up another pre-order, usually for a year.
- You lose some of your launch day mojo. When you make a sale on pre-order, your book gets a ranking boost there and then. On most other retailers, when

your book makes a sale on pre-order, it counts as a sale on the release date. That way, if you sell two hundred copies during your month-long pre-order period, on release date you get a ranking boost that corresponds to a hundred copies sold on release day. That's not the case on Amazon.

What you do depends entirely on your strategy. If you have an established series of novels, with an army of readers itching to grab the next part of the series up as soon as it's released, you may find that putting it on pre-order will get you a nice, big payout on release day. If your book is the first of a new series or a standalone, and you're a relatively unknown author, maybe a pre-order is not the way to go.

eBook Content

The second page in the publishing flow is pretty simple, so let's go through it really fast. You should have everything you need to upload to this page by now: your formatted book manuscript and your cover.

In the first box (Manuscript), select if you want to enable DRM (digital rights management) for your book. **Do not do it.** I've never done it and when I googled "DRM on Kindle books" to research why anyone would want to do it, here's the first result that came up on Google:

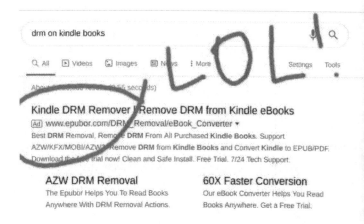

My opinion on the matter of piracy is that DRM (in any media or software product) only serves to degrade and complicate the experience of legitimate customers. Pirates will find a way to get the product for free, stripped of all the annoying BS that actual customers have to deal with. So don't enable DRM, m'kay? Whatever you do, some people are going to download your book for free. Deal with it.

After you've selected 'No' to the DRM question, you get to upload your book manuscript. KDP lets you upload the book in a ton of formats, so choose the format your book is in and select 'Upload eBook manuscript'.

You then get to upload your book cover. You get the choice of either using Amazon's Cover Creator or uploading your own cover. Almost all of the Cover Creator's templates look like the result of gastroenteritis and the only choice you're given is deciding which end they come out of. So make sure you have an appealing cover ready to upload (in JPEG or TIFF format) and select 'Upload your cover file'.

After you've uploaded both your manuscript and your cover, you get to launch the previewer to see what your book will really look like on a Kindle. **Do not skip this step**, as it can reveal misformatted content and other errors you may need to fix in your manuscript!

After you click 'Launch Previewer', you'll get a pop-up message saying that the conversion process may take a while. Does it take a while? I guess it depends: do you consider the Mesozoic Era 'a while'? Because if you do, you'll find the description pretty spot on. Don't freak out and think that something's wrong—nothing's wrong.

Go do something else: make a cup of coffee or ten. Go to the mall. Travel to Proxima Centauri in a World War I biplane. When you're back, the process will probably be complete. Check your book in its entirety to make sure that the formatting is in tip-top shape and then proceed to the next step, which lets you provide KDP with an ISBN number. There's no reason to do this for an ebook, so select 'Save and continue' to go to the third and final page of the ebook publishing flow.

eBook Pricing

KDP Select Enrollment

The first section on this page allows you to enroll your book to the KDP Select program. KDP Select requires the digital version of your book to be exclusive to Amazon but offers you various promotion opportunities that you wouldn't otherwise get.

For one, your book is included in Kindle Unlimited and the Kindle Online Lending Library. This means that readers that have a Kindle Unlimited subscription can download and read your book for 'free'. It's not actually free, because they are paying a monthly subscription to Amazon. If you're thinking 'What's in it for me?' I don't blame you. Here's the thing: every time someone reads a page of your book, you get paid a small amount of money. The exact amount varies, but it's usually close to half a cent per page. Simply put, a thousand pages read will make you about 5 dollars. Not too shabby.

KDP Select enrollment also allows you to run Kindle Countdown deals and even offer your book for free for five days for each enrollment period of three months. Kindle Countdown deals are time-based promos for discounted books, with the price of your discounted book increasing in set intervals until it reaches its original price again. This creates a feeling of urgency and can lead to increased sales. As for your five free days, you can use them to promote your book through various channels (eg. promo sites, more on these later). Keep in mind that a free download counts as a purchase, so any reviews posted by people that downloaded the book while it was free will be tagged as Verified! This is cool because it demonstrates that it wasn't your mom leaving the review. Or maybe it was your mom and she decided to support you by buying the book. Awwww.

Finally, as I've already mentioned, the enrollment period for KDP Select is three months, so it shouldn't be that scary of a decision for you: if you can't make up your mind, go ahead and place your book in Select. If you decide that you prefer to publish your ebook on other retailers, let the three months pass and then don't renew your enrollment. To have that safety net, be careful not to select 'auto-renew' when you are placing your book in Select.

Territories or, You Don't Have The Right!

KDP gives you the ability to select the territories that you'll be releasing your book in. The only reason to not choose 'Worldwide' is if you don't hold the rights to the book for certain countries in the world. In that case, select 'Individual territories' and uncheck the ones you shouldn't release the book in.

Royalty and pricing

Let's make this one easy: if you price your book between $2.99 and $9.99, Amazon will give you a 70% royalty on the price of the book. If you price your book below $2.99 or higher than $9.99, Amazon will give you a 35% royalty.

Obviously, logic dictates that you should price your books between $2.99 and $9.99 and Lady Logic is right. That's what most authors do, most of the time.

There are some exceptions to this, however: if you're running a promotion on a book promo site, it's a good idea to lower the price to $0.99 while the promo is active because many people on those sites are bargain-hunters. You won't be making a lot of money this way but that's not why you are running a promo, as we'll discuss in the chapter about promoting your book.

Authors who write books in a series sometimes lower the price of the first book to $0.99 and keep the rest of the series priced at or above $2.99. They then make their money in read-through, where they make no money on the first book (or even a substantial loss, if they are promoting it heavily) but make up for that by selling the rest of the books in the series to readers that liked the first one.

Why can't I set my book's price to free?

I know you see free books on Amazon all the time. However, you may have noticed that you can't set your book's price to free, so how are all those crafty devils doing it?

There are two ways this can happen:

1. The book is temporarily free as the result of a promotion. As you can no doubt remember (I mean, it's two pages back), if you enroll your book in KDP Select, you get five free days for each three-month-long enrollment period to use as you please. In this case, the author is using one (or more) of those days.
2. The book is permanently free or, if you want to sound cool at indie publisher parties, it's *permafree*. Listing your book as a permafree takes a little bit of commitment and maybe some luck. First, you need to list your book on retailers other than Amazon (eg. Google Play Books, iBooks, etc). Then you need to make the book free on those retailers and email KDP support to ask them to price-match your book on Amazon (ie. make it free). If the support guy's hemorrhoids aren't flaring up on that particular day, they may grant your wish.

Book lending

The last section on the last page of the publishing flow lets you enable book lending, which lets someone who downloads the book to lend it to their friends and family to read for a limited amount of time. If you price your book between $2.99 and $9.99, you're not given much of a choice: the lending option is enabled by default and it's locked so you can't disable it.

Publish it!

Hey, we're done! Hit the 'Publish your book' button and in less than 24 hours, if Amazon doesn't find anything wrong with it, your book will be live on Amazon. Congrats——get ready for the crippling anxiety attacks and constant stats checking!

Scenic detour: What about that no-content/low content publishing business I keep hearing about?

No.

OK, maybe yes.

It depends.

For those of you who don't know what it is, no/low-content publishing refers to the creation of books with a tiny amount of content or even none at all. Usually, these books are journals, workbooks, diaries, coloring books, dot grid notebooks, you name it. You create the internal layout, export as many pages as you want, slap a nice (or horrible) cover on it and then you release it as a paperback on Amazon.

If your passion is writing books, the no-content/low-content method is not going to resonate with you. It's a completely different beast and, in my opinion, it's nowhere near as fulfilling as writing an actual book.

One thing that bothers me is that the no/low-content scene has given rise to opportunistic quasi-gurus that hype it endlessly as the new way of making passive income while you're eating Nutella in your boxers and jerking off to Susanna Hoffs in the basement. I'll be right back.

In many ways, creating no/low-content books is more similar to the Merch by Amazon model, Amazon's POD platform for garments, than it is to actual book publishing through KDP. In fact, many people in the Merch community have turned to taking their t-shirt designs, resizing them and putting them on the covers of low-content books and then throwing them on Amazon by the hundreds *per day*, hoping that some of them will sell at some point.

Have I done it? Yes. I've experimented a bit by creating ten titles and publishing them through CreateSpace (which has been replaced by KDP Print). Two of them sell about once a month, which is frankly way more than I expected. It makes sense, then, that if you upload two thousand of these things, maybe you'll be making a couple hundred bucks per month.

If you don't mind stinking up your KDP dashboard with thousands of these things (that you cannot remove from the dashboard, just unpublish from the Amazon store) and want to give it a try, you'll need some covers and some PDF files for the book "content".

Making the covers is up to you, buddy. You'll need some cool display fonts and maybe some clipart and illustrations from places like The Hungry JPEG (https://thehungryjpeg.com/), Creative Fabrica (https://www.creativefabrica.com/) or more upscale outfits such as Creative Market (https://creativemarket.com/) and Design Cuts (https://www.designcuts.com/).

As for the book interiors, there's nothing better on the market than Tangent Templates (https://templates.tangent.rocks/). Tangent Templates costs $59 at the time of writing, so it's not wallet-bustingly expensive, but it's not exactly free either. It's very flexible, though, in that it's not just a bunch of static PDFs you slap together. It's an actual web app that allows you to mix and match various templates and export them to any size you want.

If you just want to test the waters and don't want to spend $59 in the process, you can go for something free, like BookBolt's Interior Wizard (https://designer.bookbolt.io/interior-generator.php).

I'm pretty sure that most of you didn't get this book to learn about no/low-content book publishing, but it's been such a hot topic lately that I wanted to at least comment on it. Personally, it feels like I'm taking an ice-cold cringe shower every time some guru makes another post or video about it, but there you go—I live to please!

Chapter 4: Promoting your book

After all your hard work writing, editing, formatting and uploading your book, you'd think that Amazon's servers would crash on release from the tidal wave of customers eager to get their cyber-mitts on your ebook.

I'm sorry I have to tell you this but, unless you have a million moms, things are likely to be somewhat underwhelming. Also, if you have a million moms you're probably a fungus or something, so a lack of book sales is the least of your problems.

With 3.4 million books in the Kindle Store at the time of writing, and many more being added every single day, you shouldn't expect to make many sales through organic discovery, ie. people performing searches on Amazon and coming across your book without any promotion on your part. It's not impossible to succeed without promotion——just very, *very* unlikely.

And, not to get too pedantic here, but whether you've succeeded or not depends on your definition of success. If you're happy with selling twenty books per month, then you could realistically reach that target by releasing a couple of nonfiction books on some popular and relatively underserved niche and doing no promotion at all.

However, if your definition of success is making it as a full-time career author, things get a little more complicated. In that case, you're going to need to spend money to make money.

There are many ways to advertise your books. Some of the most common ones are

- **Amazon Advertising ads**, also known as AMS from their old moniker, Amazon Marketing Services. You'll still hear people refer to them as AMS ads.
- **Facebook ads**
- **Bookbub ads**
- **Promo sites** such as Robin Reads, eReader News Today, etc

Now, every one of these is worth a book in its own right. Luckily, these books already exist, so here are my suggestions for each of the platforms I've mentioned

- **Amazon Advertising**: Brian D. Meeks' *Mastering Amazon Ads: An Author's Guide* (*https://www.amazon.com/Mastering-Amazon-Ads-Authors-Guide-ebook/dp/B072SNXYMY/*) is the first book I read on the subject and, to this day, it remains my favorite. It's funny, well-written and contains a ton of information that helped me, a total noob at the time, run profitable ads almost immediately. You should totally get it.

- **Facebook Ads**: OK, it's not a book, but *Mark Dawson's Ads for Authors* course is the bee's knees. The dog's bollocks. The ewok's digestive tract. The course also covers Amazon Advertising and BookBub ads (new content is being added all the time). The downsides? It's expensive and it's only accessible to new students whenever Mark decides to open registration. The downsides' upsides? You can pay in monthly installments, which makes the price much more palatable and since it's not always open, fewer people learn the secret sauce you learn from the course. The fact that Mark Dawson is a gentleman and has none of that slimy guru sheen also makes it much easier to recommend his course. If you can afford it, you'd be a fool not to enroll in it. Since I promised a book, I keep hearing great stuff about *Help! My Facebook Ads Suck!* (https://www.amazon.com/Help-My-Facebook-Ads-Suck-ebook/dp/B078NBW3M3) by Mal Cooper and Michael Cooper, though I still haven't read it.
- **BookBub Ads**: David Gaughran's *Bookbub Ads Expert* (https://www.amazon.com/BookBub-Ads-Expert-Marketing-Publishing-ebook/dp/B07P57V38D/) is considered the gold standard here and indeed it is.
- As far as I know, there's no authoritative guide to promo sites so I'm not going to suggest anything.

In this book, I'm going to focus my attention on two of these advertising avenues, which are, not coincidentally, the two I'm most familiar with and the ones I've had the most success with: Amazon Advertising and using promo sites. Even though I'll keep it relatively short, I'll try to jampack as much info as I can in the following pages, so you can promote your book effectively ASAP. Let's get going!

Amazon Advertising (formerly AMS)

General concepts 1: PPC vs CPM

AA operates on an auction model and serves PPC ads.

Huh?

If you've never advertised on the web, you probably don't understand what that means. If you have, you'll probably have your own opinion on the matter of CPM vs PPC. If you do, keep your opinion to yourself because it doesn't matter: you only get PPC ads here, and you're gonna like it.

CPM means *Cost Per Mille* and it refers to the cost of showing the ad a thousand times (a single showing of the ad is called an *impression*). Since webpages don't spontaneously load into existence, this means that the ad has been shown to customers a thousand times. Has it been shown to a thousand visitors once? Or has it been shown to ten customers, with each visitor seeing the ad one hundred times? Unless the website specifically states its policy on this, you won't know.

PPC means *Pay Per Click* and it refers to the fact that the advertiser pays only when a visitor clicks on their ad. You may ask 'What happens when a user clicks on my ad twice?' and then make the logical leap to 'What happens when some douchebag scum asshole competitor keeps clicking on my ad to drive up my costs and stop me from advertising?' I've looked into this and the best answer I got was from the Seller Central Amazon forums, where a user said this

> ***Only the 1st click from an IP address registers each day per sponsored product campaign.*** *I suppose they could still click different ads if you run multiple campaigns or change/hide their IP address and use multiple accounts to run up the total, but that requires some effort.*

Some people are dicks. Let's just accept that and move on.

General concepts 2: Important metrics in Amazon Advertising

Budget

This refers to the daily budget or the maximum amount you're prepared to pay per day for a specific campaign.

CPC

CPC stands for **cost per click** and it's the amount of money you pay every time someone clicks on your ad. You may be wondering who decides what the cost per click should be and the answer is you.

That's right, you. As I've mentioned, AA serves ads based on an auction system. This is how it goes: say that you want your book ad to appear every time someone does a search for "hydroponic cultivation in Sudan". During the ad creation process, which we'll go through together later in this chapter, you're asked to bid on that particular keyword. Remember, a key*word* is usually a *phrase* and, in this case, it's "hydroponic cultivation in Sudan".

If you decide that the maximum amount you're prepared to pay for a click on your ad is 25 cents, and some other weirdo that wrote a book about hydroponic cultivation in Sudan decides that they are prepared to pay 20 cents for a click on their ad, it's your ad that's going to appear in the most prominent place in the search results. Take *that*, Weirdo Numero Dos.

Since AA is based on an auction system, you won't be paying the 25 cents you specified when bidding for the keyword. Instead, you'll pay the bid of the second-place seller, which in this example is 20 cents. This is why you almost never pay the full amount per click that you specified.

Bidding is probably the most important metric that will define if your ad makes a positive return on investment or if it's running at a loss.

Impressions

Every time an ad is displayed on a web page, that counts as an impression. An impression doesn't mean that the ad was actually seen by the website visitor. It just means that it existed somewhere on the page. In Amazon's pay-per-click system, you are not charged for impressions, only clicks. To maximize impressions, you need to bid on a lot of keywords and you need to bid a large enough amount per keyword for your ad to appear in the search results and product pages. More on this later.

Clicks

The number of clicks on your ad, you dummy. Dividing the number of clicks by the number of impressions gives you the **clickthrough rate**, another important metric that we'll look at in more detail later.

ACOS

This refers to the **advertising cost of sales** and its expressed as a percentage. It is calculated by dividing the spend your ad has made in a specific period of time with the sales attributed to that ad in the same period of time.

An example may help clear things up. Let's say that you've spent 15 dollars between 12/09/2019 and 12/11/2019. During those three days, the sales attributed to your ad are reported to be 14 dollars. So let's divide 15 by 14 and the result is 107.14%.

You've also lost one dollar, correct? I mean, 15 minus 14 equals one. You're spent 15 dollars and you've made 14, so a loss of one dollar, *right?*

Wrong. Let me explain why.

When AA reports the sales attributed to your ad, it reports the entire amount that the customer paid to buy your book. But wait: you don't get to take home the entire amount. You get a 70% royalty for books priced between $2.99 and $9.99. Outside of that range, your royalty is even lower, a depressing 35%

In the previous example, let's say that your book costs 7 dollars. This falls within the 70% royalty range and it also means that you sold two books. 70% of 14 dollars is 9.8 dollars. Let's round it up to 10 to simplify things.

So you've spent 15 dollars on your ad but, during the same period of time, you've made 10 dollars. Which means that your ad actually lost you 5 bucks.

This is why, if you're selling ebooks priced between $2.99 and $9.99, you need to keep your ACOS below 70% for your ad to be profitable. If it's exactly 70% you are just about breaking even. If it's over 70%, your life is over and you are a massive failure and a disappointment to your parents. Good job, loser.

There is a way for an ad to be operating at above 70% ACOS and still be profitable. You'll learn about it later.

Let's make an ad!

Ready to get into the nitty-gritty of the ad creation process? Log into your KDP Dashboard and select 'Promote and advertise', which is a button next to the book you've published.

On the next page, in the 'Run an ad campaign' section, choose the marketplace that you wish to advertise in. While at the time of writing there are minimal differences between the different marketplaces, the general concepts are always the same, so select 'Amazon.com' and click 'Create an ad campaign'.

When the next page loads, you'll have to select between a 'Sponsored Products' ad and a 'Lockscreen ads' ad.

Here's something you should remember: **friends don't let friends run lockscreen ads.**

Lockscreen ads don't even run most of the time and, even when they do, the results are sub-par.

Instead, focus on the ads that can actually be profitable: Sponsored Products ads. Sponsored product ads appear in search results or product pages and can be very effective if used correctly.

Click continue in the 'Sponsored Products' section to be taken to the 'Create campaign' screen. This is where the magic will hopefully happen.

Let's take it section by section.

Settings

Campaign name

First, select a name for your campaign. My suggested template is:

[Book initials] + [date] + [type of ad] + [bidding strategy] + [base keyword]

Let's say that your book is called 'Floating Butts of Venus'. (If your book is called 'Floating Butts of Venus', stop what you're doing and email me immediately with a purchase link)

Here's how I would name the campaign:

FBoV 12/17/2019 SponsProd-ProdTarg low-bidding KWs: raunchy science fiction

FBoV stands for Floating Butts of Venus, obviously.
12/17/2019 is the starting date of the campaign
SponsProd-ProdTarg lets me know that it's a Sponsored Products ad using a Product Targeting strategy (more on this in the relevant section)
Low-bidding means that I'll be using a low-bidding strategy
KWs refers to the base keyword I'll be using to find the rest of the keywords or the products I'll be targeting.

Some of this stuff may not be making a lot of sense right now but they will soon, I promise.

Start-End

Next, you're asked to enter the starting and ending date of your campaign. We want to get it running ASAP so select your current date for Start and select an ending date that you feel comfortable with for End.

When I was starting out, I felt more comfortable selecting an ending date but as I got more experienced with AA, I made the decision to let the ads run indefinitely (ie. I left the End field set to 'No end date'). These ads are not set-and-forget (far from it), so the best strategy is to check them daily and terminate them yourself if you feel that they are not doing acceptably well.

Daily budget

How much money are you willing to spend on this ad daily? I consider $5-$10 to be a safe little budget to start with. Don't worry, Amazon won't be spending a lot of your daily budget. I currently have twenty campaigns running, each with a $10-$50 daily budget, and my average daily spend *across all campaigns* is about $5.

Targeting

This is where you select automatic or manual targeting.

Automatic will let Amazon select the keywords or products it will be targeting with your ads. It's an easy way to get started but, in my experience, not a very effective one.

Manual is where it's at: you get to select the keywords or the products you'll be targeting and, if you choose the right products or keywords, you should be getting thousands of impressions per day.

Campaign bidding strategy

At the time of writing, there are three choices in this section

- Dynamic bids - down only
- Dynamic bids - up and down
- Fixed bids

I usually go for 'Dynamic bids - down only' or 'Fixed bids'. This means that my spending never gets out of control. I've tried the 'Up and down' option a few times and the only thing that went up and down was my dinner in my esophagus when I saw how much I was spending for results that weren't appreciably better.

Below the bidding strategy selection section, you'll find another subsection where you're able to adjust your bids by placement. This means that Amazon can increase your bid by up to 900% if it means that your ad will appear in a product page or at the top of the search results. I avoid this section like the plague because it makes the entire thing too unpredictable: a $0.50 per click bidding can shoot up to a $4.50 per click bidding at Amazon's discretion. Yeah, *no*.

Ad format

There's not a lot to say here. A custom text ad will let you write some short copy (up to 150 characters) for your ad. A standard ad will simply show your ad without any extra text.

I usually go with the custom text ad option. I prefer to let people looking at my ad know what they're in for *because clicks cost money*. If your title is even slightly ambiguous, craft some text that clears things up for the reader.

For example, the previously-mentioned 'Floating Butts of Venus' could be a book influenced by Greek mythology or a science fiction novel. A short blurb will clear things up.

Here's one blurb

> *Humans have colonized the skies of Venus. But you can bet your butt nobody expected the attacking floating Butts. An explosive sci-fi epic!*

And here's another

> *Zeus has cursed Venus with the power of precognition... and a flying arsehole! Now, a lovestruck mortal is her only hope.*

Neither leaves a lot to interpretation and that's the way it should be. Do whatever you can to get people that are actually interested in your book to click on your ad or you'll be spending money for nothing.

Products

This is where you select the products that you want to advertise to the masses. If you've selected the 'Custom text ad' option, you'll only be able to select one product to advertise, since the expectation is that your custom text is meant to advertise a specific product.

If you've selected the 'Standard ad' option you'll be able to select more than one product, although in that case, you should make sure that the products you're targeting are all meant to be advertised using the same keywords.

I never advertise multiple products in the same ad because it makes the resulting data more difficult to sort through and analyze.

Select the book you want to advertise by clicking the 'Add' button next to it.

Targeting

This is the section that will make or break your ad. Nothing matters as much as this section, so treat it with the respect it deserves. The magnitude of respect it deserves is this: imagine that your mom has fused with Jesus, Socrates, and Albert Einstein and then had sex with your dad, who has fused with Confucius, Beethoven (not the dog, you sicko) and Marie Curie. The result of this bizarre union is a kid who goes on to be the first man on Mars and also cures cancer while he's there. You know how much you'd respect that kid? Well, respect this page **more**.

Automatic targeting

Let's get the easy stuff out of the way first: if you've selected 'Automatic targeting' in the Settings section we've discussed above, there's not much to do here. Simply select a default bid and you're done. DO NOT select the suggested bid, unless you enjoy dumpster diving for dinner. In my experience, starting off with about 35-50% of the suggested bid should be fine. You can modify this later if you want.

If you've selected 'Manuel targeting', what exactly has Manuel ever done to you?

If you've selected 'Manual targeting', oh boy.

Manual targeting, part 1: Keyword targeting

If you're targeting keywords, your books will show up in search results related to those keywords. This is amazing, especially on Amazon where people go specifically to buy stuff.

But what are the keywords you should target? This is where things get complicated but I'll try and break it down to you in a way that'll make a lot of sense. To do this, I'll use my book "Satan, Aliens, Go!" as an example. Before we go any further, please create a new blank spreadsheet in Excel or Google Sheets to write down the keywords we'll extract through the process I'm about to outline.

Trawl through your brain

"Satan, Aliens, Go!" is a humorous science fiction novel about Satan saving the Earth from aliens. As the author of the book, and a fan of the genre, I know that the biggest name in funny sci-fi is probably Douglas Adams, the author of *The Hitchhiker's Guide to the Galaxy*. Guess what? That's my first keyword right there: 'douglas adams'. And my second one: 'hitchhiker's guide to the galaxy'.

What else has Douglas Adams written? How about the Dirk Gently series? Hey—there's another keyword: 'dirk gently'. What are the titles of the books in the *Hitchhiker's* series? And what about the titles of the books in the *Dirk Gently* series? If you don't remember, Google them. You already have about 20 keywords to write down in your spreadsheet.

Use Google's Keyword Planner

The Keyword Planner is a tool you can access on the Google Ads platform over at https://ads.google.com. After creating an account, you'll be taken to a dashboard view, where you can access the planner by selecting Tools & Settings (on the toolbar up top) > Planning > Keyword Planner.

When you're there, select the 'Discover new keywords' option and then the 'Start with keywords' tab. Enter one or more relevant search terms in the text field and click 'Get results'.

What will come up is a list of what the keyword planner calls 'keyword ideas'. Here's a partial list of what it came up with when I ran the search. The total number of results was 104 ideas, which is pretty solid.

the restaurant at the end of the universe

douglas adams books

douglas adams dirk gently

starship titanic

douglas adams 42

douglas adams doctor who

the meaning of liff

the salmon of doubt

young zaphod plays it safe

douglas adams books in order

etc.

These keywords are based on Google searches, not searches on Amazon, but they give us a pretty good idea of what people are searching for in general.

To download them, click on 'Download keyword ideas' and open the .csv file to access the keyword list. Copy them into the spreadsheet we created earlier, in the same column as the rest of the keywords you've already gathered. There will probably be some duplicates. Don't worry about that—that's why we're doing this in Excel/Google Sheets and not in Cubase or Photoshop.

Go through your book's and related books' also-boughts

If you've released your book and you've made at least a few sales, its also-boughts can be a treasure trove of keywords. To find your book's also-boughts, scroll down until you reach the section that says 'Customers who bought this item also bought…'. I can't promise that the section will actually be there and, if it is, I don't know where it'll decide to show up but the reason it plays hard to get is because it knows how valuable it is.

Also-boughts are an amazing resource because customers that have bought your book also went on to buy those books. This suggests an overlap of interest between your book and the books on your list that you can use to your advantage.

To collect a bunch of keywords, start going through the books in the also-bought section and write down their titles and authors, *separately*. You want the title to be one keyword and the author to be another keyword. I'm going to do this for the also-boughts in 'Satan, Aliens, Go!' and write down some of the keywords I'll extract:

Outcast Marines Boxed Set

James David Victor

Not Alone: The Contact Trilogy: Complete Box Set

Craig A. Falconer

Tales of Talon Series

A.A. Warren

Interstellar Caveman: A Funny Sci-fi Space Adventure

Karl Beecher

Here are some pointers so that you can optimize your keyword collecting:

- The also-boughts list is a carousel! You can click on the arrow on the right to see another five books. And then another five. You can keep going for (at the time of writing) twenty pages.
- When you're writing down the keywords, try to sanitize them a bit. First, remove any special characters and punctuation from them. No colons, no unnecessary capitalizations and no periods—unless it's that time of the month, ladies. When people search for Terry Pratchett's Discworld books on Amazon, they don't write "Terry Pratchett's Discworld books, if you so please m'lady" in the search field. No, they write "terry pratchett discworld books" and then, to add insult to injury, they fart loudly.
- For very long keywords, try to break them up into smaller ones.

Just to give you an example, in the case of 'Not Alone: The Contact Trilogy: Complete Box Set', I'd probably drop the 'Complete Box Set' completely and remove the colon, thus being left with the keyword **'not alone the contact trilogy'**.

If your book is newly-published and it hasn't made any sales yet, you won't be able to go through its also-boughts because it won't have any. In this case, select a book that you think is very similar in content and tone to your own and go through its also-boughts for keywords.

After you're done collecting your keywords, copy and paste them in the same column as all the others in the spreadsheet we prepared earlier. If you want, follow the exact same procedure for the 'Customers who viewed this item also viewed…' section.

Use Amazon's autocomplete in product search

This one's pretty simple, but it can give you a lot of useful variations on a single keyword. Visit Amazon and start writing one of your keywords in its search bar. Amazon is going to start suggesting variations on your keyword that it knows people have been searching for. I did this for my keyword 'douglas adams' and it suggested nine variations on it.

Do this for a few of your keywords, collect the variations and enter them into your spreadsheet. Do I need to keep repeating that you should place them into the same column as all the other keywords? *Fine*: place them into the same column as all the other keywords.

Use Amazon's autocomplete in ads

When you select Keyword Targeting , you're given the choice of **Related** (some keywords generated automatically by Amazon), **Enter List** and **Upload File**.

I treat the **Related** section like I'd treat an automatic targeting campaign. If these are the keywords Amazon's suggesting I should use, it makes a lot of sense that it'd be the keywords they are using for their automatic campaigns. I usually select 'Add all' since it's more keywords for the ad machine.

Enter List and **Upload File** are pretty much the same thing, with different ways of importing the keywords. In the first case, you copy and paste the keywords from the spreadsheet, while in the second case you upload the file containing the keywords. I prefer to just copy and paste the keywords in the text field that appears when you select Enter List.

The reason I'm explaining all this a bit prematurely is to tell you about a feature of the text box I just mentioned. If you start writing a keyword into this text box, it's going to start suggesting more keywords, just like Amazon's product search did.

Use this functionality to enter more keywords for your campaign! It doesn't hurt to also enter these keywords into your spreadsheet for future reference.

Use PublisherRocket

Remember that long, tedious process that you had to go through in order to collect keywords from also-boughts? Of course you do, even though I bet you wish you could forget. What if I told you that you don't need to do it yourself?

PublisherRocket (formerly KDPRocket, https://publisherrocket.com/) can do that for you. It can also

- Suggest keywords for your store listing (y'know, those seven fields you fill before you even upload your manuscript)
- Help you discover the right categories for your ebook, to increase your chances of having a #1 New Release or a #1 Best Seller
- Compile and display info about your competition, as well as dig up dirt on them. That guy with the best selling book in your category? Pretty sure he's cheated on his wife. Or has thought about it. PublisherRocket will know. Get them to remove their book from the store by blackmailing them and become the #1 best seller yourself. Then head to Vegas with the earnings and cheat on your wife too. Then be found out by PublisherRocket and be replaced by another #1 best selling author. It's the circle of life.

PublisherRocket will help you collect hundreds of keywords in minutes. I use it for all of my campaigns with great results. In case you're wondering, I'm not affiliated with them, nor do I get a kickback every time someone signs up. I just think that it's an amazing tool that's a must for anyone who can afford it. Not that it's insanely expensive—at just $97, I'm pretty sure you've had more expensive nights out.

Remove duplicates and enter into the campaign

So you've placed all of the keywords you've collected in the same column of your spreadsheet. Time for one final step before we plug them into the Amazon ads machine.

Select the column that the keywords reside in and then

- In Google Sheets, go to **Data > Remove duplicates**.
- In Excel, go to **Data > Remove duplicates**.

Isn't it ironic how in the above description of how to remove duplicates, **Data > Remove duplicates** is itself a duplicate? Life always finds new ways to surprise you.

You now have a clean set of keywords to plug into the Enter List text field I mentioned before.

Set the campaign keywords

Just like I described above, copy and paste your keywords into the Enter List text box. Before you do anything else, make sure that you've done the following:

1. You've changed the default bid to something more sensible. I swear, one of these days the default bid will show "Your firstborn's soul and a pack of Doritos" as its price. Start low. At the time of writing, the default bid is $0.75 per click, which may not sound like a lot but shut the fuck up, Bill Gates. Set it somewhere between $0.20 and $0.35. As default bids keep increasing in price, my current suggestions may be too low in a year or two. It doesn't matter. Experiment.

2. You've selected which match type you want to use for your keywords. Here's what Amazon itself says about what each match type means

Broad: Contains all the keywords in any order and includes plurals, variations and related keywords.
Phrase: Contains the exact phrase or sequence of keywords.
Exact: Exactly matches the keyword or sequence of keywords.

I usually go for 'broad', although you can choose multiple types. Interestingly, the   combination of a keyword with a match type generates a unique keyword, which means that if you enter the keyword 'tossed salad and scrambled eggs' and then select all three match types for it, you'll have used up three of your available keyword spots per ad, of which you 'only' get a thousand.

After you've done both of these things, click 'Add keywords' and wait a couple of seconds. We're almost ready to post the ad, baby! But first, let me show you how to target specific product pages.

Manual targeting, part 2: Product targeting

With product targeting ads, you can show your book ad on specific product pages. Unlike sponsored product ads, you're not relying on keywords and user searches to gain visibility and clicks.

Instead, you tell Amazon "Here's the plan, boyo: I'm bidding this much and, should I win the auction, I want—nay, *demand*—my book to be displayed on that there product's page. Now get to it, lad. Post-haste!"

Not sure why you had to put on that ridiculous Welsh accent, but now Amazon will go and do your bidding (get it?)

This is a really granular way of targeting other products that a keyword cannot offer. To continue with my example of "Satan, Aliens, Go!", let's see what I would do to create a product targeting ad for my book.

The first thing you have to do is select whether you want to target Categories or Individual Products. You can target both in the same ad, so why not!

When you select Categories, you get a choice of Suggested or Search. Choose the suggested categories that apply to your book and search for other categories to add.

For my book, I went with

- Humorous Science Fiction
- First Contact Science Fiction
- Alien Invasion Science Fiction
- Humorous Fiction

On the Individual Products tab, I ignored the Suggested tab and went straight for the good stuff: the Search tab.

For this ad, I decided to stop targeting Douglas Adams and let the poor man rest in peace. Instead, I went for Terry Pratchett. In the search field, I entered 'terry pratchett' and let it show me the search results. Here's some advice when targeting individual products:

- **Select the products with the highest amount of ratings**. It does not matter how high the average rating is: what matters is how many reviews the products you're targeting have. This means that people are engaged with the product.
- **Always target eBooks with your eBooks and paperbacks with your paperbacks**. We're creatures of habit and once people develop a taste for Kindles, they're less likely to go for print books. Conversely, some people love paperbacks and physical books in general (and may not own Kindles already) so they'll go for your paperback.
- **You can target products other than books.** If you've written a novel about sparkling vampires and cuddly werewolves, target the Blu-ray box set of Twilight.

I targeted most of Terry Pratchett's catalog with bids high enough that would ensure that my book would appear on those product pages whenever someone visited them.

With correct targeting, the power of this type of ad cannot be overstated. If you target enough products (I'd say anything over 300 products should be fine) you'll get an enormous amount of impressions.

Negative keyword targetting

In this section, you specify keywords that you don't want your app appearing for. This may sound counterintuitive and not a little confusing, so let's cut to the chase: you mainly use this section to **stop your ad from showing up in searches for free books**. You don't want to pay for freebie hunter clicks. If they fail to see that your book actually costs money and click on your ad, you'd be getting clicks from people that had no intention of buying your book.

So go ahead and include terms like **free books** and **free kindle books** in your negative targeting.

Creative

This is the last section in the ad-creating process and if you've selected the "Standard ad" option in the 'Ad format' section, you don't have to do anything but click 'Launch Campaign' to have your ad reviewed and start seeing those sweet, sweet dollars start rolling in. Or out. It depends. Let's talk about it later.

For now, we have to talk about what happens if you've selected the "Custom text ad" option. In this case, you're given 150 characters to sell your book to the customer. Think of it as an elevator pitch for your ebook.

As you're probably aware, 150 characters is not a particularly long amount of text. I've had farts that lasted longer than that, so you have to use the available space wisely.

But what do you write?

Let's start with what you *don't* write. Amazon really hates the following:

- Mistakes in spelling, grammar, and syntax ("This is teh bestest book!1!!!1!")
- Unsubstantiated claims ("The best crocheting book throughout the multiverse")
- Swearing ("Fuck yeah, this book is the best, asshole, cunt, tits")
- References to price or to the book being in Kindle Unlimited ("30% off its regular price")
- Sexual innuendo and double entendres ("If you like your books long and hard, you'll love this one")
- Drugs and drug abuse ("Shooting up heroin is good for your cholesterol levels")

Since the book cover is automatically part of the ad's creative, you must also avoid these on your book's cover:

- Boobs, vaginas, bare-chested Adonises, sexually-suggestive outlines and silhouettes, women in lingerie (unless it's Amish lingerie or something), etc
- People holding guns pointed towards other characters on the cover or towards the reader. I'm not joking, even though it probably sounds like I am.
- Cigarettes, alcohol and illegal drugs. These guys are no fun.

For more info on what is allowed in the copy of the ad and on the cover of your book, go to https://advertising.amazon.com/resources/ad-policy/en/book-ads

Now let's see what you should write. If you follow these tips, your ad copy should be at least passable:

- Same as with the book description, **make sure to start with a hook**. Make it a very short one: six to seven words, max.
- **Don't mention character names**. Possible exception: your protagonist.
- First sentence is your hook. **Second sentence should be your sales pitch**.
- There are a couple of good ways to write your sales pitch: you should either mention what makes your book special or what *doesn't* make your book special.

Let me explain that last one because you're probably staring at the page wondering if I'm mad.

Mention what makes your book special by zeroing in on its unique selling point or main characteristic. If your book is really scary, point that out by calling it *horrifying*. If your book is an intense thriller with your protagonist in constant peril, call it *harrowing*. If your book is funny, call it *hilarious*. Forget modesty: really go for it.

What doesn't make your book special refers to the technique of describing your book in terms of other books or works in general: your book is 'Dan Brown meets Lee Child'. 'Late Douglas Adams meets early Terry Pratchett'. 'Transformers meets Sleepless In Seattle'. 'Like Jurassic Park and Slaughterhouse-5 had a baby'.

Here's actual ad copy for "Satan, Aliens, Go!" that did really well

> *A fleet of invading aliens. A former King in exile on Earth. Douglas Adams meets Terry Pratchett in this hilarious romp through spacetime!*

Once you've written your ad copy, click 'Launch campaign' to submit your ad for review.

Monitoring your ads

Creating an AA ad is pretty straightforward once you've got the hang of it. I can easily throw together an ad with 500 keywords in ten minutes or less and you should be able to do the same pretty soon if you keep practicing.

Creating an ad is only part of the equation, though. If you want the result of the equation to be in your favor, you're going to need to monitor the ads you create closely. Amazon ads are *not* set-and-forget. If you're not willing to monitor the ads daily (or at least three times a week), don't waste your money on them.

Monitoring the ads is essential for the following reasons:

- To make sure that the ads are running. If they are not getting impressions (AKA eyeballs looking at them), they are not.
- To make sure that you're not overspending. I know, there's a daily budget limit. So what? Why should you spend $5 a day for nothing?
- To make sure that the ads are actually doing what you want them to do, ie. sell you some books.
- To make sure that your ads are still working. Over time, ads that used to work splendidly tend to become less effective.

Monitoring impressions, clicks and sales

After your ad is approved, you should wait at least 24 hours before you start monitoring it. Sometimes ads take a little time to get going, so don't sweat it for a while.

Has it been a day? Good—time to start looking at your impressions. Most people agree that you should be getting at least two thousand impressions per ad per day, one click for every thousand impressions and one sale for every ten clicks your ad gets. If you're not getting these results, don't worry. I've never seen any conclusive evidence that this is what you should be shooting for.

Visit your AA dashboard and take a look at the table. Set a date range (or select one of the predetermined ones; I usually go for 'Today' or 'Yesterday' since I monitor my ads daily) and take a look at the number of impressions your ad got. If it's still early in the day, your number of impressions is going to be low so don't worry. If you're looking at the results for an entire day, you should ideally see a number between 500 and 2000. The higher, the better.

If you're getting below 500 impressions per day, there's a problem. You want to have a lot of impressions because they cost you nothing and it means that your ad is being shown to customers. **If your number of impressions is low**, here are the two things that could be wrong with your ad

1. **You are bidding way too low**: A low bid is relative, with variations between different marketplaces. At the time of writing, a $0.10 bid won't get you far in the Amazon.com store, while a similar bid of £0.10 in the Amazon.co.uk store could get you a decent amount of impressions. I'd say that, right now, bidding $0.20-$0.30 per click is fine, as far as the US store goes. However, these things change, so always experiment with your bid by starting low and then raising it in increments of 5 cents if you're not seeing a lot of action (ie. impressions). My rule of thumb is to divide the suggested bid by three and start bidding at that level, ie. if the suggested bid is $0.75, I will start bidding at $0.25 and sometimes even lower than that.

2. **You are not bidding on enough keywords**: If you are bidding on fewer than a hundred keywords, prepare for disappointment, even if you're bidding relatively high. You need to use the methods I outlined in the Manual Targeting section to gather a lot of keywords. Go for at least three hundred.

If you are getting a decent amount of impressions but **no clicks**, here's what's almost certainly wrong:

1. **Your book cover sucks balls**: Hairy, disgusting balls. People take a look at it and think 'Nope. Not with a ten-foot pole'. *Fix your cover.*

2. **Your ad copy is horrible**: I know it's only 150 words, but you can still mess it up. Follow the instructions I gave you earlier in the book to try and fix it. If you want to, you can run two versions of the ad, with

different copy for each and even run a standard ad with no ad copy at all and compare their performance. This is called an A/B test in online marketer parlance.

If you are getting a decent amount of impressions *and* clicks but **no sales**, look into the following:

1. **Your description is not optimized for conversions**. There's an entire section in this book about optimizing your description. Refer back to it to make your description more attractive to prospective buyers.

2. **Your 'Look Inside' makes people wish they hadn't looked inside**. Every book that has been self-published on Amazon via KDP has a 'Look Inside' label on the cover on the book's page. People can click on the cover and read some of the book (about 10% of it) in their browser. If your book's formatting, syntax, grammar, and core content sucks for ten percent of its length, readers will make the not-entirely-unreasonable assumption that the rest of the book sucks too. Even if none of those things suck, you still have to make sure that your book has a strong start and/or an intriguing premise that will draw readers in.

Optimizing your ads

When I started running my first ad campaigns on Amazon, I treated them as monolithic structures, to be left running if they were making money or to be terminated if they were losing me money. So I would create them, let them run for a week or so and then decide their fate. It wasn't a bad plan but I was missing some very important details.

For one, I knew that I could adjust the bid by keyword but I considered that to be too much work and I never did it. Little did I know that this was the secret to more successful campaigns.

Visit your ad dashboard and click on one of the ads that you've created and that has been running for more than a week. If you still don't have one of these, create it right now and come back to this section once you've let it run for a week. On the left side of the screen, you should see a column with the words 'Ads', 'Placements', 'Targeting' and so on. Click on 'Targeting'.

Change the date range to 'Lifetime' and prepare to have the veil lifted from your eyes.

Have you been making any sales from this ad? Which keywords have been responsible for your sales? Do these keywords have a favorable ACOS?

PRO-TIP

You can sort these values by ascending or descending order by clicking on their column title once or twice.

Here are the things I look for and how I deal with the information I gather from them:

- Most of your impressions and clicks will be the result of a small subset of your keyword list. Many keywords won't get any impressions and/or clicks at all. Let them be. You never know, they may become the new hotness thanks to a trend in the future.
- Are there any keywords that have more than 10 clicks but have never sold a single book? I usually terminate those keywords, unless their cost per click is very low (between $0.02 to $0.12 per click)
- What's the ACOS for the keywords that are actually selling me books? If it's over 80%, I lower the bid for those keywords by $0.02 to $0.05 increments. There's only one exception to this, which I'll discuss later.
- If the ACOS for a keyword if below 60%, I'll raise the bid price for it in $0.02 to $0.05 increments. For example, a book with an ACOS of 11% gives me a lot of leeway for raising its price, so I might raise its bid price by $0.05 or even $0.10. If a keyword has an ACOS of 50%, I need to be more conservative with my bid increase, so I'll raise the bid price in increments of $0.02.

This strategy pretty much ensures that your campaigns will eventually become profitable. And here's a keyword for ya: ***eventually.***

Because make no mistake: you have to be prepared to spend some money experimenting and doing keyword research before your campaigns are optimized for sales. Do not consider that money wasted: you're spending it to build a keyword library that you'll be using for years and to learn a valuable skill that'll help your career as a self-published author take off.

To summarize:

- Monitor your ads daily.
- Adjust the bids for individual keywords as you gather more data about clicks, sales, and ACOS.
- Never give up, baby!

The Over 70% Exception

I've been mentioning an exception to the 'Anything over 70% ACOS is unprofitable' rule and it's time to reveal what it is.

It's pretty simple, actually: if you have a series of books, you would normally only advertise the first one, especially if it's a fiction series that has to be read in order to make sense. If your ACOS for the ad for the first book in the series is over 70%

but you're getting decent read-through (people buying the rest of the series after they finish the first book), your ad may be profitable.

Here's an example. Say you have a trilogy. The first book is priced at $2.99, and the second and third books at $3.99. If it takes you (on average) ten clicks to make a sale and each click costs you on average $0.25, that means that you're spending $2.50 to sell a $2.99 book. Subtract from that Amazon's 30% and you're spending $2.50 to make about $2.00.

Or are you?

If your books are engrossing, addictive reads that connect to each other, you can expect a lot of readers to purchase the second and even the third book in the trilogy. In fact, after they've purchased the second book, the chances of them buying the final book in the trilogy skyrocket. This means that the $2.50 that you spent to make the sale of the first book might end up making you $2.00 (first book) + $2.74 (second book) + $2.74 (third book), which is about $7.50.

My point? Don't be afraid of high ACOS percentages when you're advertising the first book in a series. The longer the series is and the stickier the books are, the bigger the chances that your ad is actually profitable. Of course, always verify that your ad is profitable by following sales of books in your series before and after you run the ad. Any increase in sales after you run the ad(s) should be attributed to it.

Promo sites

Why use them?

As things are drawing to a close, I'd be remiss not to mention promo sites.

Promo sites are websites that maintain mailing lists of (usually) loyal readers that, more often than not, are looking for a bargain. Usually, these are voracious readers that don't want to spend more than $0.99 for a book (or even a box set of books) because they read more of them in a month than most people read in a lifetime.

Different people have different opinions on these sites, with some refusing to use them and some claiming that they are an integral part of their launch strategy. I fall into the latter camp. In fact, I fall so hard into it that I almost break my legs daily.

People that refuse to use them have usually been burned at least once, either by using a dodgy site for their promo or by having the wrong expectations for their promos.

The purpose of these sites is *not* to make you a quick buck. In fact, you'll probably make a short-term loss by using them.

Why should you use them, then? For two reasons:

1. **To rank higher at launch**. Remember the categories research I had you do earlier in the book and how, if you choose carefully, you should not have any trouble getting the #1 New Release or even the #1 Best Seller badge? That won't happen automatically. Getting a boost from a promo service or two will help you get there without having to beg your Facebook friends to buy your book, 'it's only $0.99, guys'.

2. **To make The Algorithm notice you**. Amazon's algo is like that super-hot girl in high school that would only notice guys that were already popular. Your postmodern revenge fantasy thriller set in 17th-century Ottoman-ruled Sparta, currently sitting at #987,145 in the Kindle Store because you released it without any promotion (and also probably because it's a postmodern fantasy thriller set in 17th-century Ottoman-ruled Sparta—let's be real here) will not show up in any search results and will not appear in any 'Books you may be interested in' emails sent by Amazon to its customers. To stretch the high school analogy to a breaking point, your book is the nerdy, gassy kid that's into Lars von Trier and The New Pornographers, sitting at the back of the class being a little creeper, doing littlecreepery things. You need to keep a steady stream of sales happening for some time to maximize your book's chances of establishing itself as a book that The Algorithm will consider eligible to fuck. I'm sorry, I meant *promote*.

3. **To sell your first in a series at a steep discount**. Selling your first book in a series at $0.99 during the promo period will not make you an immediate profit but it's quite possible that you'll make a profit from people reading the rest of the books in the series (this is the *readthrough* we were talking about) that you'll keep priced at $2.99 or even higher.

Why maybe not?

Do not use a promo site if you hope that you'll make an immediate profit using it. I mean, *you might*, but you most probably won't.

Firstly, to do well when you run a promo, you'll need to discount your book down to $0.99 or even make it free for the duration of the promo. If you discount it to $0.99, you'll be making around $0.35 per sale—not an effective way to make a profit, especially after you've paid for the promo itself. If you make your book free for the promo, you won't make any profit per download.

Secondly, even if you do well with a $10 promo, you'd need to sell at least 30 books at $0.99 to break even. Imagine how much harder it's going to be to break even if you paid $65 or even $100 for the promo.

Promo stacking

Promo stacking is the practice of running a lot of promos concurrently, in order to sell books consistently, climb up the rankings and stay there for a while.

As is always the case with selling stuff on Amazon, people have speculated about how the promo stacking should occur in order to suck up to The Algorithm more effectively. Currently, most people believe that you should start with the least effective promo services for a couple of days and bring in the big guns on the final days of your promo period. This, supposedly, pleases The Algorithm but I personally also sacrifice a goat in its name, just in case.

Let's say that you'll be promoting your book for five days on various promo services. If you do your promo stacking correctly, your sales should look like this

5, 10, 23, 50, 89

Not like this

6, 0, 20, 3, 1

Again, this is all speculation, but it's the best we have to go on right now.

Promo services

These days it seems like everybody and their dog and their dog's ticks is running a book promo service. But which ones should you trust? I've used many, and in this section I'm going to share my experience with some of them. It should be said, though, that different services will work better for certain genres. Also, keep in mind that if you're writing romance or thrillers—the genres *du jour*—you'll probably do better than people who write nonfiction or sci-fi.

Here are some of the services I've used over the years, with a short overview of my experience with them.

Bknights

(*https://www.fiverr.com/bknights*) - *base price: $5*

This is a service on Fiverr and, for the price you are paying ($5), it's a pretty cool one. You can promote both free and discounted books and I'm using them for every single one of my launches.

BookSends

(*https://booksends.com/advertise.php*) - *starts at $20 and can go up to $250 depending on genre and placement*

BookSends has done great for every genre I've advertised in. It's more expensive than the el cheapo services but it's worth it.

BargainBooksy and FreeBooksy

(https://www.bargainbooksy.com/ & https://www.freebooksy.com/) - start at $30, can shoot up to $200 depending on genre

An amazing couple of services, for discounted and free books respectively. BargainBooksy does great but FreeBooksy does amazingly well. Highly recommended.

ManyBooks

(https://manybooks.net/author-services) - $29 for their newsletter promo, $39 for their permafree promo

ManyBooks does pretty well for me. I've never regretted using them and even though they haven't been one of my heavy hitters I still use them for every one of my launches since I found out about them.

BookBub

(https://www.bookbub.com/welcome) - starts at an arm and a leg, can end up costing you your firstborn child

BookBub is the king of promo services and they know it. They reject about 80% of the books that are submitted to them so don't be discouraged if they reject you multiple times. I still haven't been able to book a promo with them.

On the bright side, according to people that have gotten BookBub promos, a feature with them can be career-defining and it will make back the money you pay for the promo and then some. So keep trying.

They tend to favor wide releases (ie. releases on Kobo, Apple Books, Google Play Books, etc) and not just Amazon exclusives. They also prefer longer books and books that have already gotten some reviews. This means that a short new book that's in KU (Kindle Unlimited) is not likely to be picked up by them.

BookBarbarian / Red Roses Romance / BookAdrenaline

(https://bookbarbarian.com/why-advertise/ &
http://redrosesromance.com/why-advertise/ &
https://bookadrenaline.com/why-advertise/) - between $25 and $35

BookBarbarian and its specialized siblings are amazing places to advertise and they always deliver. BookBarbarian advertises sci-fi & fantasy, while Red Roses Romance advertises romance (this paragraph brought to you by Captain Obvious) and BookAdrenaline advertises thrillers and mysteries.

BooksButterfly

(https://www.booksbutterfly.com/) - starts at $100, can go as high as $400 for indies.

Now, this is a strange one. Some authors claim that they are scammers and they avoid them like the plague. I disagree: I don't think that they are scammers and I think that, at most, you should avoid them like a common cold. And even then, not always.

Look, their author-facing website looks like ass. The reader-facing sites that they are running look like ass with a really nasty fistula spitting out pus in regular intervals. And yet, their free plans (as in, plans that promote free books, nothing is free about BooksButterfly itself) have done pretty well for me, even if I expected more for the prices they are charging.

They also have a reputation for being litigious with people that are saying negative things about them on the internet. Look, I'll come clean: the only reason I've included them in this section is so I could make ass jokes at the expense of their websites. Sue me. (I wasn't talking to you, BooksButterfly owner)

Want more? Here's more

RobinReads (https://robinreads.com/author-signup/)

EReader News Today
(https://www.ereadernewstoday.com/bargain-and-free-book-submissions/)

Fussy Librarian
(https://www.thefussylibrarian.com/advertising)

AwesomeGang (https://awesomegang.com/)

eBookDiscovery (https://www.ebookdiscovery.com/)

All of these have performed at least adequately for me, so visit them and check them out when you run your promos.

Why run promos for a free book?

I wanted to address this question before we move on to the next chapter. In many ways, it seems counterintuitive that you'd pay money to advertise a free book.

Amazon has two types of best-selling book lists: one for paid and one for free books. If you're giving away your book for free, no matter how many times it's downloaded, your book won't appear in the Paid list so you won't get the coveted #1 New Release or #1 Best Seller badge.

Bummer, huh?

Yes, but also no. While you won't be eligible for those badges, there are some cases in which advertising your free book with a promo service can have a very beneficial effect. Here they are:

- The book you're giving away is a first-in-series. The benefit is obvious: increased sales for the rest of the books in the series, especially if the free book is a catchy, addictive read.
- You need verified reviews for your book. When someone downloads your book for free on Amazon and then reviews it, their review is marked "Verified", same as a person that actually purchased the book when it was a paid release. Verified reviews carry more weight in the eyes of shoppers (and, according to legend, in the eyes of The Algorithm) so you want as many of them as possible. Reviews you get from ARC services (more on them in the final chapter of the book) are not verified.

There's something else I've noticed but take this with a grain of salt, as it's my personal experience, with no actual evidence to back it up: during the transition from free to paid, if your book has ranked high enough in the Free charts, it appears that it gains a visibility advantage *somewhere*. I haven't been able to track down the source of this; it may appear more often in the search results or it may appear in the Paid list very briefly while the transition happens. One thing's for sure, though: I always get increased sales in the days following a free promo and there have been times that a complete flop of a book came back to life and became a regular seller after a particularly successful free promo.

Getting reviews

General info

This chapter is going to be quite short because there's not much to be said about the subject. Here's what's clear:

You need reviews.

You don't need a million reviews. You don't even need a hundred reviews. But you need to have at least 5 reviews for your book on Amazon. A book with no reviews has no social proof attached to it. People won't take a chance on a book with no reviews, written by some guy that they know nothing about, especially if the guy looks like this

If you're thinking "No problem, I'll just get some of my friends to write glowing reviews on Amazon and Bob's your uncle", just stop. First of all, Bob's not my uncle and he *never* will be but more importantly, this could lead to the suspension or the termination of your account. Don't ask me how Amazon will know, but they will: one day you'll wake up full of spunk and energy, ready to kick the day in the teeth and crush it like a bad mother, until you find out that the reviews on your books have vanished without a trace and you're left a whimpering mess of snot and saliva, curled in the fetal position in the shower of your mom's basement. Oh, and you forgot to turn the water on so now you're a disgusting blob of shapeless organic matter and despair.

The problem is that if you sit there and wait for reviews to crop up organically, you'll be in for a long wait. Most people in the self-publishing community suggest that, on average, you'll get one review per 1000 free downloads or one review per 100 paid downloads. Sucks, right? So what are you supposed to do?

Here's some ideas.

Ask for reviews in the book

And don't be shy about it. Ask twice: once in the book's front matter and once in the back matter, after the reader has finished reading the main content. Say something like "If you'd be so kind, I'd really appreciate an honest review for my book on Amazon" and place a link to the book page right after this text.

Use an ARC service

ARC stands for Advance Review Copy. These services will send copies of your book to readers that are interested in reviewing it.

None of the legitimate ARC services will guarantee a certain number of reviews and they certainly won't guarantee positive reviews either, as that would be against Amazon's policies. Their readers are sent a copy and are encouraged to leave an honest review, without any incentivization. They are also encouraged to mention that they received a free copy for review purposes in their review.

Be careful with these services if your book is in Kindle Unlimited / KDP Select. Mention that your book is in KU and let them know that they should not offer your book for direct download. Instead, they should have their users request a copy and then send it to them via email.

Here's a couple of reputable services that you can use to increase your review count.

BookSirens

https://booksirens.com/ - *flat fee of $10 for every book accepted, after that $2 for every person that downloads your book*

Easy-to-use, with a modern interface and quite cheap to boot. It can take a while for you to start seeing reviews but they claim that 75% of the people that download a book leave a review. From my experience, that percentage is entirely accurate. You can select a ceiling for the number of people that can download your book so that you won't exceed your budget. Highly recommended.

Hidden Gems Books

https://www.hiddengemsbooks.com/arc-program/ - *$20 flat fee per book submitted which covers you first ten readers, additional fee of $3 for every additional reader, max charge of $400. 50 reader minimum order.*

The most well-known ARC service on the market, and for good reason. More expensive than BookSirens and good luck booking a spot with them before the heat death of the Universe (at the time of writing, they are completely booked for the next ten months) but they are pros and the results speak for themselves.

Resources

Talking to other people

Sure, this book is freakin' awesome, but sometimes it helps to speak to someone if you need some guidance and/or encouragement in your self-publishing journey.

For more advice and tips, don't hesitate to contact me at sebastian212000@gmail.com. I can't promise that I'll have the best, wisest answer to your question but I promise to answer any and all emails related to self-publishing to the best of my ability. If I take too long to answer, please send me a reminder email. Sometimes I get stuck in the toilet.

If you need honest, no holds barred opinions about your cover, description, manuscript etc. you need to visit the Writer's Cafe at kboards:
https://www.kboards.com/index.php?board=60.0

Kboards is also the place to look for cost-effective editors and cover designers. Unlike other forums, people are encouraged to advertise their services and there's even a thread called Kboards Yellow Pages, which is a directory of all the members that are offering their services to authors through Kboards.

There are also some, ahem, *lively* discussions going on at all times, so you can rest assured that you'll never get k-bored on Kboards.

Books you should absolutely read

Mastering Amazon Descriptions (https://www.amazon.com/Mastering-Amazon-Descriptions-Authors-Copywriting-ebook/dp/B07NSH2QLM/) and *Mastering Amazon Ads* (https://www.amazon.com/Mastering-Amazon-Ads-Authors-Guide-ebook/dp/B072SNXYMY/) by **Brian D. Meeks** are hilarious, highly informative tomes of wisdom that you need to read.

How to Write a Sizzling Synopsis (https://www.amazon.com/Write-Sizzling-Synopsis-Step-Step-ebook/dp/B01HYBWOF6/) by **Bryan Cohen**

Write Faster, Write Smarter (https://www.amazon.com/gp/product/B074CJPMZ1) by **Chris Fox** is an awesome series of books that deal with most aspects of self-publishing.

Self-Publishing Unboxed (https://www.amazon.com/Self-publishing-Unboxed-Three-year-No-bestseller-Sustainable-ebook/dp/B0762Q1ZRN/) by

Patty Jansen is pretty amazing. Patty is also a regular on Kboards!

I wasn't going to suggest any books about craft since this book is mostly about the technical aspects of self-publishing but I have to make an exception for **Janice Hardy**'s *Understanding Show, Don't Tell* (https://www.amazon.com/Understanding-Show-Dont-Tell-Builders-ebook/dp/B01M0BE4UP/) and *Understanding Conflict* (https://www.amazon.com/Understanding-Conflict-Really-Means-Builders-ebook/dp/B074FYY5SX/). Both are must-reads if you are writing fiction.

Courses

Most people are a bit wary of courses and, after having spent $700 on a course that should have honestly cost $50 for the value and amount of content it provided (and was insulting in that it blurred huge portions of the screencast out, showing an astounding lack of trust towards people that spent a pretty penny on the course), I'm pretty suspicious of them too.

However, there's a guy that has proven to be a beacon of integrity and knowledge and he's called **Mark Dawson**. His courses at https://selfpublishingformula.com/ are expensive but *absolutely* worth it. You can also pay in monthly installments, which brings the courses within the reach of most people. I've taken his Ads for Authors course and it transformed my sales in the span of a month. And, before you ask, I don't know the guy personally and this is not paid advertising; his stuff is simply phenomenal, so I'd be doing you a disservice not to mention it.

Dave Chesson also has a free course on Amazon Advertising (https://kindlepreneur.com/ams-book-advertising-course/) that you should watch. Don't let the 'free' part put you off, it's really high-quality content.

Software

PublisherRocket (https://publisherrocket.com/) is the fastest way to find a ton of keywords for your Amazon ads. I can't imagine not having it anymore.

BookReport (https://www.getbookreport.com/) or DataSprout (https://datasprout.co/) are great tools for visualizing your sales over time. Nothing essential but they are nice tools to have and they both have free tiers.

Podcasts

If you commute often, there's no better way to consume content than to listen to it, especially (pro-tip) if you're the one doing the driving. I never let a trip go to waste: I have my favorite podcasts downloaded and ready to go on my phone. Here are my favorites about self-publishing:

Mark Dawson's *Self-Publishing Show podcast*
(https://selfpublishingformula.com/spf-podcast/)

The Creative Penn by **Joanna Penn**
(https://www.thecreativepenn.com/podcasts/)

The Book Marketing Show by **Dave Chesson**
(https://kindlepreneur.com/podcast/)

The Career Author Podcast by **J. Thorn & Zach Bohannon**
(https://thecareerauthor.com/podcast/)

The Sell More Books Show by **Bryan Cohen & Jim Kukral**
(http://sellmorebooksshow.com/)

Taking my own advice

Do you know how I said that you should ask for reviews in the front and back matter of your book? Well, here you go: *if you've enjoyed the book (or even if you haven't) please leave a review for it on Amazon.* It matters a lot, not just for visibility and social proof but also because it always makes me giddy to see that someone took the time to not only read my book but also took two minutes to let me know how they felt about it.

Again, don't hesitate to contact me at my personal email at sebastian212000@gmail.com. It's always a pleasure to talk with you guys.

Until next time,

Antonis.

Appendix

THERE IT IS.
NOW GO PUBLISH YOUR BOOK!

Made in the USA
Las Vegas, NV
30 September 2021